T Skills Blueprint

9 Essential Assets to Improve Your Communication, Win Friends, Build Self-Confidence and Make Connections with New People

DAMIEN REED

TABLE OF CONTENTS

INTRODUCTION

Is this book for you? If the following situation sounds even slightly familiar then you will benefit greatly from what's to come: You wake up on a Monday morning, take a shower, finish your morning routine and get dressed for work. You take the bus to work and check your social media feed in the meantime. You're not really sure why you do that, since you barely post anything, instead you use social media as a way to see what other people are doing with their lives and feel connected to them, in a way. You get off the bus and make your way to the office. You sit in a chair and spend the next 3-4 hours doing something that you most probably don't like or at least don't enjoy doing. Lunch break comes around, you go outside to get lunch, or maybe even stay in, if your office has a cafeteria inside, find a place to sit down on your own and check your social media feed. You avoid contact with your coworkers unless absolutely necessary. Why – because they don't like you and you don't want to be up in their faces all the time asking for attention. This may sound harsh, but then Friday comes around and everyone is talking about their plans for the weekend. Your plans – stay at home and do the exact same thing you have been doing all week long. Why – because your poor social skills are limiting your interactions with other people, which is, in many ways, ruining your life. I am by no means saying that you need to be the center of attention all the time, like that one guy from work. What I am saying is that you need to have adequate social skills, which will help you develop your own social circle, where you will feel comfortable, where you will be respected and valued for who you are, where you won't just be waiting for your turn to speak – your own sanctuary of social freedom. This might sound like a dream to some of you, but believe me, it is very achievable.

You may have been told before that you are introverted and that's why you find it difficult to communicate with others. Being introverted is indeed a real character trait, however, introverted people enjoy being alone or in the company of very few individuals and they do so by choice, not because they're forced into it. Social skills are just that – skills. Nobody is born with the gift of being a great woodworker. They spend years honing that skill to become the best at their craft, so why should social interaction be any different? Although it is underestimated to the point when it is considered incomprehensible, learning social skills is extremely possible and it's not even hard! All you have to do is read this book and act out on the principles I will list in the following chapters and you will be a wizard of social interaction in no time!

I think that this is a good time for me to introduce myself, before I go any further. My name is Damien Reed, I'm 38 years old and I'm a motivator by profession. What is a motivator? Think of me as a life coach. I help people hone their social skills, offer an alternative opinion on matters that may be troubling you in your daily life and provide guidance for those that need it. Over the past 10 years, I've helped countless individuals become better versions of themselves, which is what life is about, in my opinion.

So what makes me qualified to answer your questions about social skills and actually teach you how to improve them? I don't have a fancy Ph.D in some field of psychology and won't delve deep into your subconscious to look for answers. No, I'm just a regular guy, who over 12 years ago was in the exact same boat you're in right now and decided to make a change. I didn't want to be the person with social anxiety anymore, I didn't want to have a friend circle of 2 and an acquaintance circle of 10. I wanted to be like that guy Joey from college, who was the star at every party, who everyone wanted to hang out with.

What did I do about it? I started reading books, going to countless seminars on self-improvement and consulting professionals in the field. I was a reader of practically every single blog that was somehow related to self-improvement that existed at the time. I was desperate and I needed a change, NOW!

Spoiler alert: it took a bit longer than I had hoped it

would. Over the next year, I spent every single available minute of my time looking for answers and I found them. Please note that I say "them", instead of "it", because the topic we'll be discussing in this book is complex and there is no one-step solution to all of your problems, regardless of what anyone tells you.

So why am I writing this in the first place?

I am a passionate person by nature. I have always been at the top of my class and spent many hours at home studying. Obviously, that didn't help my social skills one bit, but the point I'm trying to make is that my passion has now been focused on helping others and doing my very best to reduce the number of people, who have the same issues that I had, by as many as possible.

In this book, I have compiled my experience from all those seminars, blogs, books and meetings with professionals, as well as my professional experience from the past 10 years in an effort to do two things:

1. Save you money, because all those things come at a price. I personally believe that physical and mental care should be free for everybody, however that is unlikely to

happen anytime soon, therefore I'm writing this book as an assembled guide for a fraction of the price you would otherwise have to pay.

2. Teach you all of the necessary skills for you to become a master of social interaction, thus increasing your quality of life. Improvements in the social skills of an individual have been linked to reduced risk of depression, higher stress tolerance and many other medical benefits.

Now keep in mind that this book is not the only solution to your problems. I previously stated that there is no one-step solution to any problem in this world, let alone something as complex as our personalities. The information that follows is a compiled list of what I believe to be of utmost importance for your improvement, however simply reading it will do you no good. What you have to do is actually use the tips that I will share with you and practice using them until they become second nature you. Don't think that just because you know something you are actually using that information. Think about all the different articles about all those different diets that you have read – has simply reading them helped you lose any weight? No – they might have given you the information needed for you to then take action, but no piece of information in this world will do anything for you, unless you actually go out, get the needed experience and practice until what you're trying to learn becomes something that you do naturally.

Another thing to be noted is that actually learning to use these principles takes time, so the sooner you start – the better. I recommend that you practice the techniques we will discuss further down in their order – for example, you read chapter one, you try to incorporate the techniques and information given into your daily life. Once you start getting the hang of things, read chapter 2 and so on.

If you are motivated to change your life, this book will serve as a holy bible for you to use as guidance on your journey. Use the information, experiment, go out of your comfort zone and prepare to embark on the journey of your life, which will take you places, which you have only ever dreamed of going to.

Enjoy the rest of the story, my fellow students, and best of luck!

WHY IMPROVE YOUR SOCIAL SKILLS?

At this point it might be tempting to think something along the lines of: Well that's all great and all, but why should I take the time to actually improve my social skills? My mom always told me that I should study French in high school, I never did, and here I am.

While it is true that there is nothing fatal in life, poor social skills are, in my opinion, one of the worst drawbacks a person can have in their lifetime. Think about all the great experiences you have missed, because you were, for some reason, too scared to attend the events? How about all the missed opportunities that you could have received, if only you had spoken up at that brainstorming your company did last month, but you weren't sure you would make a convincing enough point? And the list goes on, but the most important thing you should take out from this is that lacking social skills or not mastering them can often times lead us down a path with no opportunities and no new experiences, which can seem impossible to get away from.

Still not convinced? How about this, in this chapter, I'm going to share with you some of the best reasons I think make investing the time to master your social skills worth every single minute.

1. Choosing the right people

Have you ever been in a situation where you're forced to interact with certain people, just because they're the only ones that will spend time with you? Think about the last time you went out with some colleagues from work, who you don't particularly like, but you sort of tolerate and the only reason you did that is because they're the only ones inviting you to go out. This is something that we can all relate to. And I bet that during that same evening out, you were thinking about how you could've spent your time in a number of better ways, with much more interesting people, if only you could somehow get to them. This is one of the main reason why so many people reach out to me and say, "Damien, I really wish I could go out with this guy from work, he's a top performer and attracts a lot of attention. It seems rather weird, but even though we work the same job, he makes significantly more money than I do and is always meeting new and exciting people. How can I do the same?"

At this point the answer to the above question should be obvious to you – improve your social skills. Once you get better at communicating with people, you will be the one they will want to go out with. Why? Because you will be able to hold a conversation that is not only present, but entertaining. You will meet with different people from different backgrounds, who will expand your horizons as well as you theirs. It really can't be understated how much of a difference your conversational skills can make to your day to day life.

2.   Make more money

This can be controversial to some people, but believe me – it's true. When you go to an interview for a job, most companies will have a range that they are prepared to offer for a given position. If you have worked on your social skills and know how to ace an interview and position yourself carefully, yet strategically, you are much more likely to receive an offer for significantly more money than someone who hasn't. For example, in my early years, I had a rather boring job at a printing company. I was still in college and that was the best that I could do at the time. However, a few months into my job, I found out that one of my coworkers, who was studying in the same university that I was and had no previous experience, just like me, was being paid roughly 40% more than I was. At the time I remember thinking that this situation was unfair and that the corporate world was giving more to some and taking from others. That's not the case. You see, I was much too agreeable then. I desperately needed the money and I jumped at the first opportunity available. Since I hadn't researched any alternatives, I walked into that interview thinking that no matter what happens, I have to get that job. And I did, but for significantly less money than they were prepared to offer me. I was simply undervaluing my own skills and contribution to an employer. Why was I doing that? Because I was this shy, unconfident kid who had no idea how the world worked. If I had read this book then, I bet I would've been paid even more than my colleague.

3. Build more and higher quality relationships

For this particular example, a relationship will be focused more on the business side of things than intimate ones. With a great social skill set, you will be able to strategically lay out your particular skills in front of the right people. Let's say you're a great craftsman, specifically, a woodworker. You're trying to build your own business by doing custom projects for individual clients. However, you find that whenever you go out with friends, you never bring up the topic and this way – never reach new potential customers. This doesn't mean that you should try selling to your friends directly, however informing them about it in a professional manner may result in surprising new connections made. One of them may have a friend, who renovates houses and could use the help of a woodworker. That friend, on the other hand, probably has many more friends who renovate houses or are in the construction business in some way and can open up a whole new avenue of work for you. Don't be afraid to share your passion with the world – it can't do you any harm.

4. Increased happiness, decreased chance of depression

During a study conducted in 2015, researchers found that with the rising popularity and widespread usage of social media, depression rates in children and teenagers have grown by as much as 30% for the time period between 2010 and 2015. Depression is a serious issue that can affect many people that you know, yet you may have never noticed. This doesn't mean that social media is all bad, however the study suggests that there is no replacement for actual human communication from a physiological standpoint. A high quality conversation can be just as entertaining as watching a YouTube video, but in order to have that high quality conversation, you need to work on your social skills first. The issue is made even bigger due to the fact that more and more people lack the ability to express their emotions in person. They can post countless photos on social media with tags about the way they're feeling, yet it's not uncommon to see a group of teenagers, who have gathered together and are all on their mobile devices. This isn't simply a social issue; it's a completely real medical one. Next time you have a few hours of free time, go outside with a friend, have a cup of tea and talk about something that you both find interesting.

5. Social abilities can be more important than academic knowledge

While both social and academic abilities are important, recent studies suggest that people with highly developed social skills are much more likely to achieve what they considered to be "success" than those with academic skills. The reason for this, researchers believe, is that a great set of social abilities results in more social interactions and relationships formed – therefore more opportunities presented and also the general assumption that people with great social skills are much more likely to jump at an opportunity than those without.

It is important to keep in mind that "social skills" doesn't refer to the ability to make friends or form intimate relationships alone. The term primarily refers to our ability to navigate social interactions of different character and be able to consider the different outcomes from said interactions and their consequences. Furthermore, the decisions we make that only impact us are extremely rare, if not non-existent, which makes understanding social interactions and navigating them properly all the more important.

6. You will improve your self-confidence

Although this is more of an actionable step we will discuss in the next chapters, it is also one of the primary reasons why you would want to take the time and improve your social skills. Having a realistic sense of self-worth and a matching self-confidence will result in quality relationships. Saying that self-confidence is important would be an understatement. Many people go through life without really living it to the fullest just because they lack the confidence to take that extra step or maybe take a risk. Having the ability to realize your actual worth to society is key when it comes to making decisions.

7. You will become an efficient team member and/or leader

When it comes to working as a team, social skills are one of the main precursors to success. A team project mainly revolves around the first part – the team. And one cannot possibly hope to be an efficient part of a machine (such as a team) without being able to properly communicate their ideas and visions to the other team members. We've all been in the situation, most probably in school or university, when we're assigned a project with a group of randomly selected people. There's always one member of the group who does nothing and one who does the majority of the work. The reason for that is rather simple – the leader of the group doesn't have the necessary social skills to properly guide the members and assign the tasks to each of them. Although this situation is frustrating when we're in school or university, it can be detrimental once we begin working and even worse if it's our own business we're facing those challenges in.

8. You will learn to thrive in social situations without knowing anybody

We all know how frustrating it can be to set up an appointment with a friend of yours only to have them not show up. This situation can then go in one of two ways – you either go home, feeling disappointed or, if you've mastered social interaction, you can use the opportunity to socialize with new people. Let's say you agreed to meet at a bar or a club. Once there, with your newly found freedom of speech, you will be able to create conversations with complete strangers and make the most out of your night, since you took the time to get ready and go out anyway. You might be surprised to learn that most of these encounters can form new friendships that you never would've expected to find. I personally prefer bars as a socializing place, because clubs tend to be far too noisy and crowded.

Now that you know about the main reasons why you should improve your social skills, I'm going to share my personal story with you. I already told you the story of my boring job at that printing company earlier. Naturally, after I found out that my coworker was being paid more than I was, I quit shortly after. Then a period of frustration followed, during which I was struggling to find a new job that was close to my university and would accommodate my hours. That situation was resolved for me when a friend of mine told me about this thing called affiliate marketing. But not that digital affiliate marketing we're familiar with today – but a partnership program with a local company making cookware at the time. At first, I was skeptical – after all, how much money could you make reselling someone else's products without putting your own profit margin on them? Well, it turns out you could make a lot of money with commissions up to 30%. I was immediately hooked. However, at first I was struggling to make any sales at all. I would often go up to a potential customer and the conversation would drift into some topic that had absolutely nothing to do with selling the cookware. I found myself in another conundrum. This was the pivoting point for me. I understood that in order to make money at this job, I needed to improve my ability to communicate with clients and get my point across in a way that is not too intrusive and will result in a sale at the same time. I took two weeks off of university and spent that time sitting at home all day long reading all the books that I could find in the library on elementary psychology and social skills. There weren't many e-books available at the time, so I had to rely on those sources at first read over 12 books during those two weeks. After that, I wrote up a game plan. I would go out and talk to customers using a different technique from the books that I had read each time. That didn't pay out too much either, because, like I said – there is no one step solution to social interaction. I spent the better part of the next three months making little to no money, but I was encouraged, because my average conversation time with a client had jumped dramatically. I then took another two weeks off and I tried to refine my game plan – I took into account all the interactions with clients that I had had over those 3 months and I sorted through what worked and what didn't. Again, I went out and oh my god – I made 4 sales in my first 3 hours at work again. Within a month, I was making more sales than any of my colleagues were and they started flocking to me like birds to a bag of seeds. They wanted to know my secret and I shared it with them openly. Initially, the laughed at me, but the following month, I nearly doubled my sales and made over 10000$ in commissions this month alone. That was a shockingly large amount of money to make from a part time job. All of a sudden, those books that I had read and my careful strategy creation had paid out. I was far from done, however. I spent that money on seminars and one-on-one meetings with different coaches, trying to further improve my understanding of social interactions. Shortly after, I was offered a job as a car salesman, where in my first month, despite knowing absolutely nothing about selling cars, I made more sales than anyone else in that particular dealership had for the past 10 years.

I was a rock star, riding a wave of success and earning a lot of money while doing it. Naturally, my colleagues became envious of me and started coming to me to ask for advice, despite the fact that I was the new guy and then it struck me – what point is there in me taking all this time to learn how to do something if I wasn't going to share my knowledge with anybody else? So, I did just that, I started a mentoring agency and well, here I am today. Over the past 10 years, I've spoken at over 100 seminars on many different topics, I've helped over 1000 people develop their social skills and today, together with my team, we've created this book, which I consider to be the pinnacle of my career. Not because writing a book is something exceptionally hard, but because my knowledge and experience will finally be available to a wider audience, which is what I've wanted all along.

Enough chit-chat, though, it's time for chapter 3, where we will begin discussing how you can actually do what I did and become a better version of yourself

ASSET 1 - KILL YOUR INSECURITIES AND CONQUER SELF-CONFIDENCE

I'm going to start the actual education process with this particular chapter, because I believe that self-confidence is one of, if not the most important aspects of social interactions. If I were to start with any of the other techniques and you had a self-confidence issue than you wouldn't be able to apply what you learn properly.

When I started learning about social skills and how to improve them, I was not particularly self-confident. In fact, if I have to be honest, I was about as unconfident as I could be in myself. The reason for that was simple – I wasn't particularly great at my job, which didn't offer much opportunity for me to showcase my actual skills anyway; I was doing about average in university, because

I had to work to support myself and my personal relationships were of poor quality. I was spending time with people that I didn't really want to and most of our conversations revolved around things that I was generally not interested in. For instance, at one point, my self-confidence was so low that I developed what's known as social anxiety – I would be genuinely afraid of social interactions and I would avoid them at all costs. As you can probably imagine, this development didn't really help my situation at all. I could only bear going to work and university, because I didn't really have to talk to anybody for prolonged periods of time and when such a situation came around, I would literally escape by making up some stupid excuse why I couldn't be there at the time.

Looking back at things now, I can tell that I had a textbook version of social anxiety disorder, which is a very real condition affecting millions of people worldwide. With the rise of social media and the glorification of the perfect human image reinforced by it, it's not really a surprise for anybody that this is happening. We spend hours each day in front of a screen looking at edited photos of other people, who are rewarded for looking good by receiving likes. Don't think that their life is perfect, because most of them are doing it exactly for that gratification they get. To some extent, everyone living in the modern world has a social disorder or one kind or another, in some it's more intense than in others. What I'm trying to say is that there is nothing to be ashamed of and if you believe you have a social disorder, you should look for a professional to help you deal with it. If you would rather have a go on your own, here are a few tips that can help you with that:

1. Don't let negative thoughts bring you down

If you're ever in a situation where you feel that speaking up or engaging in that social activity in any way will make you look stupid or you will humiliate yourself, banish those thoughts from your brain immediately. This might sound hard to do, and it is, but it's also extremely important. Every time that you let your negative thoughts overcome you, you're essentially reinforcing this type of behavior, saying that it's ok to be scared. The more times that you do this, the more natural it will become and the harder it will be to break free from that vicious cycle. When you catch yourself bringing yourself down, take a moment and reflect on those negative thoughts, analyze them and do your best not to get involved in the same thoughts again. Don't make the assumption that others are generally negative towards you, because they really aren't. Most of the time it's your own negative attitude that they're reflecting and projecting back to you. Be the first to make a change and you'll be amazed at how quickly the behavior of others towards you will change as well.

2. Stop thinking only about yourself

When you're in a social situation with a group of other people, say a discussion of some sort in class or during the break in university, stop focusing on yourself and start thinking of yourself as a part of the group that you're in. There are many people surrounding you and if each of them was thinking the way you were, nobody would speak and the awkward silence would become eternal. Instead, try to focus your attention on other people – compliment someone on their choice of clothes, make-up or whatever you can think of. If you're discussing something with your peers, really try to listen and digest what others are saying so that you can then make a valuable contribution to the conversation with your opinion on the matter. Also, try and be present every moment during the interaction. Don't think about what someone might say when you leave, because you did this or that. Instead, focus on the present and try to enjoy your time with these people and who knows – they might enjoy theirs with you, too!

3. Face your fears

This may sound like a cliché, however here's a real life example that I faced when trying to improve my social skills. I was particularly afraid of social interactions in public places that had no structure – such as an evening out in a bar. I realized that my fear of this situation was disproportionate to the actual threat that it posed and decided to do an experiment with myself and confront my fear by doing something I would consider unthinkable. I went out to the middle of this bar, where there was a karaoke system in place, took the microphone and started singing my favorite song. It was living on a prayer, by Bon Jovi, which is rather ironic, because I was also praying I wouldn't get kicked out with laughter. Now I'm not a particularly great singer and I'm by no means anywhere near Bon Jovi's level. Yet, despite me shaking the whole time, it turns out I was the first person to ever step up and take that microphone. After I stepped off, I was greeted with a huge round of applause, not for my singing skills, but for my bravery. The owner of the bar bought me a round of drinks and put my name on the wall of fame as the first person to ever use the karaoke machine. I was instantly faced with this huge amount of attention from all sorts of people in bar, who suddenly wanted to talk to me and it felt AMAZING! Now this might be something you wouldn't be comfortable doing and honestly, I wouldn't advise you to jump into the deep like I did. Instead, start small. Ask a co-worker to go out after work, make small talk in social situations. Baby steps in general, but once you feel the change, don't be afraid to go out and do something drastic like I did.

4. Make physical changes to your lifestyle

This might sound weird, but the way that you choose to live your life can also affect your anxiety issues. Try to exercise more, as exercise has been linked to reduced stress levels and increased serotonin levels – you know, the happy hormone. Limit caffeine and other stimulants, which might further make you uncomfortable. Drink in moderation and make sure you get enough high quality sleep.

The next step you should take is to eliminate worry from your life. That sounds simple, after all, who wouldn't want to be as free as a bird, not worrying about a single thing in life? I know I would. Completely eliminating worry is not actually possible, but you could do that for the small things. Worry will not bring anything to your life, except for some unwanted side effects, but it certainly won't help you anticipate the outcome of a situation. It will make you dread that same outcome. How do you do that? Research shows that worry, unlike some other aspects of anxiety related disorders, is common is most humans. However, it is especially harmful if you suffer from an anxiety disorder. There are methods to reduce worry, backed by science. Here are some of them:

I. Separate the things that are actually worth worrying over from the ones that aren't. This will help you understand that, most of time, your problems aren't really problems to begin with and you can solve them rather easily. If you think it would make it easier for you, write down the things that worry you and try to think over them in a logical manner.

II. Ask yourself if your thoughts are productive-this is something that you should be doing with all things in life, but especially your thoughts. If you find yourself worrying over a particular issue, ask yourself if worrying will actually help you solve anything or if it's just clouding your mind. Once you find yourself in a state of confusion and unproductive thought, do your best to discard those thoughts immediately and focus on something else that will actually improve your quality of life.

III.   Trying to anticipate future events isn't bad, obsessing over them is. There is no problem with you thinking about the future and planning ahead, just do so in a reasonable manner. If you find yourself dreading something in the future, accept that right now, there's probably very little you can do about it, or if there is something you can undertake that will resolve that future problem, go out and do it, instead of sitting around worried.

IV.   Set aside a time to worry. Sometimes, worrying can actually be productive, because it tends to keep us grounded. In order to avoid compulsive behavior related to worrying, set some time aside for when you have no immediate tasks at hand and, well, worry away. Once the time is up, however go about your daily business and leave worry behind. This tip can be particularly useful for people with serious worry issues, especially if they tend to mess with your general plan.

V. Reduce time spent in front of a screen. Research has shown that spending increased periods of time in front of a digital screen can lead to increased feelings of anxiety and worry. The reasons for that are still unknown, however there was a study done a while ago, which suggested that spending time in front of a screen kicks our brains into a sort of overdrive mode, which could explain the feelings of euphoria and even mania in some cases. Nevertheless, it's a good idea to cut down on your screen time and enjoy the outdoors a bit more.

VI.   Don't be too harsh on yourself - Another recent study shows that the increased levels of anxiety and worry may also be linked to our generally higher expectations when compared to previous generations. Nowadays, success is visible everywhere, which makes all of us try to achieve it and sometimes, overachieve. We tend to set unrealistic goals for ourselves and when we fail to meet those same goals, we get disappointed with ourselves, which – surprise, surprise – doesn't help our feelings of worry.

So let's say you've done all of the above with decent success. The next step we're going to discuss is how do you actually know you've achieved something. More particularly, we're going to talk about what true confidence feels like versus superficial confidence. The key difference between the two, definition wise, is that superficial confidence is what you might run into if you haven't overcome your anxiety issues yet and try to make it look like you have. There are a few issues with this. I recently read an article on the "Fake it until you make it" trend in California, where certain people would fake being rich in an attempt to make others believe they are and buy their products. This may work for businesses, but it most certainly won't work when it comes to your confidence. The reason is rather simple – people will see right through it. Putting on a mask may feel like deception, but it rarely is. I've met very few people, who can actually pull it off. The others, most often, end up looking a bit silly. So how do you know if you've achieved true confidence? A confident person is relaxed. They're not pushing their presence on anyone – they understand their value and qualities and don't try to force themselves on others who don't necessarily enjoy their company. A confident person is calm in most situations – they won't start a fight, unless it's their absolutely last resort. They take the time to truly listen to you – they understand that there are other important people, apart from themselves, and will take their time to get to know you before making a decision whether they like you or not.

I remember the first time that I realized I was confident enough. I was in a meeting with a client of mine and, usually, I would get extremely anxious before those meetings as I was, in a way, afraid that I wasn't good enough. So, I was in this meeting with a client, who was very important to my future career. He brought good business to our car dealership and getting him interested in our new line was crucial. I was sitting there, calmly, taking my time and walking him through the details without a single moment, where I had lost my breath or a single "bathroom break", when I would stare at myself in the mirror encouraging myself. I was relaxed, at ease and, most importantly, I knew that I was good at my job and that I was doing my absolute best to make sure he was satisfied. After the meeting was over and the paperwork was signed, he came up to me and said: "You've changed quite a bit. I remember seeing you during one of my previous meetings here, you were the shy guy at the back of the room and look at you now. Way to go, kid!" His words meant the world to me, as it was the first time I had received such a praise from someone, who I looked up to. I didn't become full of myself, however. Instead, this only encouraged me to pursue my goals ever harder and give it my all.

So here are the steps that I took to become confident. Follow through with them and you'll be a master of confidence yourself:

1. Visualize

Visualization is a very important tool in many trades, yet when it comes to improving your confidence levels, it's often overlooked. Try to imagine yourself in the absolute best version of yourself you can picture. Then, do this every single day and do everything in your power to get closer to that image, day in and day out.

2. Go out of your comfort zone

Don't be caught up in the routine of your daily life, doing the things you know that you can. In order for step 1 to be effective, you need to push further and further. The way to do this is only by doing things that make you uncomfortable, even scary at times. Remember that story I told about the bar? Do something that you don't feel comfortable doing every single day and you'll soon enough be afraid of nothing.

3. Set realistic goals

The main reason why so many people fail at many aspects of their lives is that they set unrealistic goals. If you try to lose 50lbs of fat but only lose 20, you count that as a failure, when, in reality, it's a win. Set smaller objectives and update them on a regular basis to keep yourself on track.

4. Offer a helping hand

Sometimes, helping others helps us more than them. The feeling that you get out of doing something is unbelievable. Feel grateful for what you have and give as much as you can back.

5. Learn to say no

Learning to say no is a rather complex task for most people. They believe that if they reject somebody's request, that person will be offended. In reality though, a request is just that. The definition of a request contains the possibility of it being rejected and if someone gets offended for that – it's their fault, not yours. Say no, respect yourself so others can respect you.

6. Take the time to make yourself look good

I doubt it that there is any scientific evidence to support this claim, but it's what has helped me the most throughout my period of dealing with anxiety. Take the time to groom yourself properly, dress cleanly and neatly. You don't have to spend thousands of dollars on clothes, but wearing a clean and tidy set goes a long way in making you feel good and after all – that's what confidence is all about.

7. Increase your credibility

Lastly, I would like to mention that when it comes to confidence, the best things that you can do is educating yourself. When you're the smartest person in the room it's hard to feel unconfident. Take the time to read a new book, go to a seminar or start a new course at university. Do whatever you can to educate yourself and it will pay off, big time.

Don't forget that all the steps and advise described above are only going to be effective if practiced regularly. It might help to set some time aside each day to practice these new skills that you obtain and make sure that you keep them online. When you go out, try to use as many of the techniques discussed, because the more you use them the more they become natural to you. After all, nobody becomes confident by sitting in the back of the room reading a book with advise. You become confident by going out and practicing what you read in that book.

There is one other trait that confident people tend to share, which we haven't spoken about yet – rejection. A confident man is not afraid to be rejected and he pursues what he desires, regardless of how many times he would have to be turned down.

One Friday night I went out with my colleagues from the dealership to celebrate this week's sales. It was supposed to be nothing out of the ordinary – go out, get a few drinks at the usual place and relax. However, it turned out to be the most extraordinary evening of my life, the one I met my future wife for the first time. I was smitten by her beauty so much that I really wanted to get to know her. I walked up to her and introduced myself immediately, before anyone else had the chance to get to her. She laughed. When I asked why, she simply smiled and said: "I've never seen anyone look so confused at first and so happy shortly after". We spoke for hours that night and I, being a young and bold guy, decided to try to take her home with me. She wasn't willing to though. She rejected me and on top of everything, gave me a fake phone number. That's the oldest trick in the book, I know, but I wasn't willing to give up. I only had a name and a club, where we went to. Luckily for me, the club kept a guest list, mostly for their convenience but as it turns out – for mine too. I spoke to the manager the following day and he gave me her full name. I spent days looking for her and I finally found her workplace on Facebook. Cyberstalking, I know, but I wasn't willing to give up. So what did I do? I went to her workplace on Monday afternoon with a bouquet a flowers and left it with the receptionist with a note saying: "I already got your phone number from the lady at the front desk, here's mine in case you want to fight back." She called later that day. We'll expand more on that story in the dating chapter, but what I want you to take home from this is that there is absolutely no reason for you to be afraid of rejection. It's not like it's the end of the world. And if you really like the person and want to expand on your relationship with them, never give up. You never know what might come out of it, if you don't try.

Here's a homework assignment for you: Walk up to a friend or colleague and make a ridiculous request. As ridiculous as you can think of. Why? Because this will help you understand that rejection is nothing to be afraid of. Ask your classmate if you can borrow their car and take it across the country. Ask a coworker if you can use their desk at work to eat your lunch at, because you don't want to make crumbs at yours. Improvise, but keep them as ridiculous as possible and you not only won't fear rejection any longer, but you will slowly but surely gain the self-confidence you have always desired.

ASSET 2 – THE POWER OF POSITIVE THINKING

So now that you've become a confidence improvement machine, how do you use your newly found confidence? Let's imagine the following scenario – you're entered into a new television show, where all you have to do is survive through the elimination rounds. They're all done at a random principle. 30 initial players and every round, one player is selected and eliminated at random. It's just you and another person in the final round and you have your fists clenched so tightly in excitement that you almost break your fingers and the other player wins the big prize - $100k. You, however, get the second place award, which is $50k. How would that situation make you feel? Most people would say that they're rather disappointed that they didn't win and feel sort-of sad. This doesn't make any sense, does it? They've just won $50k, that's more than some people make in a year! Yet, they still fail to see it because they're blinded by the negative thought of losing. Even though the possibility of you winning that 2nd place prize is only around 3% and you're extremely lucky to be in that position, you most likely feel you could've done better.

In philosophy, there are three main types of outlooks on the world around us – skepticism, realism, and positivism. There's a famous analogy used to describe these three outlooks – the half full half empty glass expression. It refers to the way people look at things – a realist would say that the glass is full of 100ml of liquid, for example, because they observe and draw a conclusion based on facts. A skeptic would say that the glass is half empty and a positive thinker will say that the glass is half full. If we transfer the above example to this scenario, we can see that most people tend to think skeptically – they don't appreciate the fact that they've just won $50k, because they lost out on winning $100k.

So what difference does it make? – you might ask. The difference is rather simple – thinking positively allows us to enjoy the events that happen around us to the fullest, regardless of how grim they might seem to somebody else. In the scenario listed above, the person we described doesn't get to enjoy their 50 thousand dollar win, because they were disappointed by not winning the 100 thousand reward. In an alternative scenario, however, where the person is optimistic, they would be perfectly glad to take those 50 thousand and enjoy it.

So what exactly does positive thinking mean? It surely can't be just enjoying whatever happens in life. Positive thinking refers to thinking positively not only about events that have already happened but also about those that are about to come and envisioning them, thus creating the energy and drive needed to make those visions become a reality. We spoke about visualization in the previous chapter and this is an extension to that.

The benefits of positive thinking are numerous, and the movement, in general, has recently gained quite a lot of popularity with a lot of businessmen and CEO's quoting it as a motivator for success. The list of positives is rather long so here are a few of them I consider to be the most important

1. Mental health

- The topic has been researched heavily, especially in recent years and there has been a lot of emphasis on it. It's considered to be as important as physical health nowadays and positive thinking is a surefire way to better your mental state. Small changes in your lifestyle, such as this one, can have a huge impact in the long run so they mustn't be underestimated

2. Job success

- thinking has been linked to reduced stress levels and increased stress tolerance, which are both parts of our careers. Everything is stressful nowadays, especially our careers. The job marketplace is more competitive than ever and employers no longer look for job-related skills alone, instead, they want healthy individuals that can tolerate high-stress levels and still get their job done. Positive thinking is bound to help you manage this aspect of your life.

3. Relationships

- talk a lot about relationships in this book and that should be no surprise to anybody. If you think about the relationships that you have at the moment, there probably aren't too many happy-go-lucky people that you know. However, if you do know any, you are familiar with the influence they can have on others and how they're the most beloved people and often referred to as the "heart" of the party. Positivity goes a long way with people, regardless of the situation that you're in.

4. Resilience

- thinkers have consistently shown higher levels of resilience in recent studies. To put this simply, you're much less likely to have a breakdown if your attitude about life is generally positive. Crisis management becomes easier, the chances of having a panic attack are significantly reduced and your overall quality of life improves dramatically.

- it comes to applying positive thinking, giving direct tips can be rather difficult, because everyone is in a different situation. Instead, I'm going to share my list of things I believe you should avoid when trying to think positively.

5. Guilt shaming

- shaming or guilt-tripping is a practice used by some people in an attempt to force guilt onto others because they don't like the outcome of a particular situation. This is a practice to be avoided at all costs since it leads to no gain for any of the parties. Instead, you should accept that not everything will go your way and that's fine. Express your wants and desires properly and you'll be okay.

6. Having the last word

- have undoubtedly seen this in some people. They will do whatever it takes to have the last word in an argument or a fight in an attempt to show the other party that they are dominant. However, in most situations, it remains just that – an attempt. More often than not, this is a cover-up for their insecurities and other people acknowledge that and generally let them have the last word, but it's never a pleasant experience.

- you can do instead: understand that people are intelligent in their way and that nobody likes being put down and made to feel inferior. Avoid this practice and listen to people, if an argument ensues, try to turn it into a discussion instead.

7. Manipulation

- manipulators are witty individuals, who will do absolutely every and anything to make things go their way. What's worse is that manipulators will often be extremely subtle when forcing you to conform to their will and it may take months or even years to understand them. There's not much that you can do about people trying to manipulate you, apart from being suspicious, but don't ever resort to manipulation.

8. Gossip

- is the devil's language. I remember reading that somewhere a few years ago. It's not far from the truth since gossip is easily turned into a habit and furthermore it can be transferred from person to person in a matter of minutes. Gossip is simply hurtful to everybody involved. Even if what you're gossiping about is true, it probably violates the subject's privacy and is not something that a classy, confident person like you would ever do.

9. Having bad manners

- a strong belief of mine that manners make the man. A person without manners is like a car without wheels. Its engine can run and it can theoretically perform some actions, but it's utterly useless and unproductive. Take the time to educate yourself in proper manners, even etiquette if you can. If you have to, take a course on the subject and believe me, people will notice this about you from the very first moment.

I'm now going to share a personal story of mine to illustrate just how powerful and life-changing positive thinking can be. I already told you about my job at the car dealership and here's a situation I had to face when working there. We had just started selling a new brand of cars, I'm not going to share names, but they were in demand at the time. The manufacturers told us that they were allowing us to sell their cars as a favor and we needed to meet a certain deadline by the end of the year. That deadline was ridiculous. I was already pretty high up in the hierarchy of the dealership, so I was present at that particular meeting. They also informed us that if we do not meet that deadline, they will no longer supply their cars to us, because "the demand is higher than we can supply and we need to make sure our cars are being sold in the most efficient way possible", which for today's market sounds insane, but things were a bit different back then. Now they had come in with the attitude of the alfa, thinking that they could boss us around. This wasn't acceptable, because the terms of that agreement were astounding and we needed to find a way to agree with them. So what my boss and I did is we requested a break from the negotiations to discuss a few things. We went into our office and my boss was all over the place panicking. This was very untypical of him, but I suppose every man has his limits and he had a lot to lose. I kept my wits about me and told him to calm down and think rationally. There were two options – we could either give up or we could come up with a solution of that would potentially resolve the issue. We started thinking, but, unfortunately, we didn't have much time. John, the dealership's owner, said something about having to miss out on the deal, which he had to pull so many strings to get in the first place.

- Well, why don't we go from there? – I said
- What do you mean, Damien?
- We're one of the few dealerships in the state that are being allowed to sell their cars, right?
- Yes, that's true.

- And we need to meet that deadline to keep things that way.
- Yes.
- Am I the only one seeing the potential solution here?
- Well, I'm not seeing it so, yeah, you must be.
- What if we leveraged the fact that we're the ones allowed to sell the cars and resell some of them to other dealerships? We keep the deal, the manufacturers are happy, because their numbers are out of the factory, and we're going to make a lot of money in the process. Sure, we might have to sell to dealerships at slightly lower prices, since they have to make a profit too, but the cars are so highly demanded right now that we could leverage that and still make a profit for our dealership
- My boss was suddenly stricken – we could pull this off.
- Jesus Christ, Damien, you're a genius! – he said.

I'm not telling this story to boast about how great of a

car salesman I was, but rather to show you that no situation in life is inevitable and positive thinking can take you a long way to getting the best possible outcome. Long story short, we finalized that deal and made a lot of money in the process. However, what's important here, is the fact that positive thinking led the negotiation process further. If I wasn't thinking clearly and positively, we would never have closed that deal and, probably, our dealership would've lost the opportunity to sell the brand shortly after. At the end of the day, positive thinking saved us. We had a really big Christmas party later that year to celebrate that.

This chapter is all about positivity, so I think I should end it on a positive note as well – be kind to yourself. Even if your progress isn't as linear as you had hoped it would be, give it some time. Go for a nice walk, clear your head and get back to work. You can do it!

ASSET 3 – PEOPLE LOVE A GOOD LISTENER

This is probably the most controversial topic we're going to discuss in this book and there's a simple reason for it – listening isn't a topic that people pay attention to, at all. We all just assume that it's a built-in skill that we all have and have mastered long before we've even realized we could communicate with other people. After all, from the very first moment, we're born, we listen to everything around us and it only makes sense for us to think there's no room for improvement. However, that's not the case. Listening may be a built-in skill, but you would be surprised to learn that, most of the time, we listen passively. We engage in a conversation and unless the conversation is particularly interesting or informing to us, we tend to let the other person speak while waiting for our turn to do so. This is the primary reason for miscommunication between individuals – we react poorly to statements we have misunderstood and we have only misunderstood them in the first place because we listened passively. There is a fix to that and it's called active listening. Listening is using our hearing sense to receive language or other sounds and interpret them via our brains. The problem is that this process requires our focus, attention, and energy to interpret the sounds of words and process them properly. To visualize this more vividly, imagine sitting in a dark room with no distractions whatsoever. You would be able to pick up every single sound coming from every single source. Or, when you live in a house for some time you start to recognize the individual screeches that your doors or floors make when someone interacts with them. On the other hand, if you're watching TV or scrolling through social media while talking to someone, your attention is divided and therefore your listening ability worsened. You may be thinking that this isn't true for you, but believe me, it is. Every person's brain has a limited ability to process a given amount of information per a given amount of time. Dividing that attention between two or more sources of information reduces the quality of the information received.

So, what has this got to do with your social skills? Well, in this chapter, we're going to discuss what active listening is and how you can use that skill to improve your communication with people. Before we dive into the technical stuff, however, I would like to give you one more example of why active listening can change your communication with others forever.

Imagine the scenario where you and a friend have sat down to have a cup of coffee and catch up. You haven't seen each other for months and have a lot to talk about. The conversation starts fine, your friend tells you all about their affairs over the time that you haven't spoken and shares some interesting facts about his life. Then, they ask how you've been during that time and you begin talking about yourself. Meanwhile, you notice that they pull their phone out and begin answering to some messages or scrolling through social media, or whatever else they may be doing. The great conversation you were having just a minute ago has now turned into a monologue where you're talking and they're just saying "Mhm" or "yeah, I know". This is a very common situation in modern societies and is a key contributor to poor social skills in people. You see, in this particular scenario, you would feel frustrated. After all, you listened to their story actively, you asked questions, you showed genuine interest and now they're just looking at their phone not paying any attention to you whatsoever. In some extreme cases, you might ask them an absurd question and you would still get the same reply. They are listening to you, their hearing sense is working perfectly, but they're not paying attention to what you're saying because their attention is divided between the conversation with you and whatever else they may be doing on their phone or laptop or whatever device has taken their attention away from you. It's unpleasant to be on the receiving end of such treatment, but it can be even harsher if you're the one treating people this way because you'll see them slowly creep out of your life and find others to share their experiences with, who are genuinely interested in what they have to say. Nobody likes losing friends, especially if it's over something as simple to fix as this.

So, how do you correct this behavior? Active listening is a term that refers to the process of listening with all of your senses and engaging with your communication partner, but also being seen doing those things. A good example of active listening cues would be eye contact, asking questions relevant to what the other person's talking about, sharing personal stories related to the topic of discussion and genuine interest in the conversation. Keep in mind that interest in the activity at hand can be communicated not only verbally, but also using body language, which is even more important.

Listening is, in my opinion, the core component of a healthy social skill set. Regardless of how good you may be at all the other topics, we're discussing in this book, failing to listen to what others have to say will never result in meaningful relationships. It's not something that just happens, you have to really be involved in the conversation and also, adhere to the unwritten rules of conversations. What are these rules? Here are a few:

- Remain neutral when listening say you're having a conversation with a friend about their work problems. You must remain neutral in the early stages of the conversation, even if you disagree with them on some points. After all, you're listening to them and not the other way around.

Be patient

- when talking about emotional topics, people tend to make short pauses to catch their breath or to formulate what they're trying to say properly. These pauses should be accepted and not taken as an invitation to give your opinion on the matter. Give the other person the time they need to say what they want to.

Wait for the answer

- you ask a question regarding the topic of discussion, wait for the other person to finish their answer before asking a second question, even if you want to. The reason for that is simple – it makes them feel unheard and as if the only thing you were interested in was gathering pieces of information, instead of sympathizing with them.

Don't contradict unless completely necessary

- listening to a story, you may notice that people tend to bend a few details to make the story more appealing. That's normal, pretty much everybody does it. What's not okay to do is to interrupt the person talking to correct something that they have said, just because you wanted to. This not only makes them lose credibility, but it ruins the flow of the story as well, so essentially you're spoiling it for everyone. Now there are exceptions to this rule, where the person talking may be misleading people or trying to trick them into believing something that simply isn't true, which might be a good time for you to interfere.

- it comes to listening, there are also a few tips that I'd like to share, which will make you a great listener:

Reinforce positively

- you're listening to a story about personal achievements or attempts at such, always provide positive reinforcement, even if the achievement may be minimal. This is a sign that you understand the effort the other person has put into making that particular thing happen and are stimulating them to progress further.

Remember the details

- isn't something that you could implement immediately, but when listening actively to a conversation, we tend to remember some key details that other people might have missed out. You would be surprised at the amazement in people's eyes when you bring those details up at a later time. We automatically assume that others won't remember those details and tend to appreciate it when somebody does.

Reflect

- you haven't fully understood something, try paraphrasing it and ask if you've understood the concept correctly. This will not only make sure that you're getting the right information but will also let the speaker know that you're attentive.

Listen for ideas

- you're listening to someone else speaking, you'll find ideas popping in your head connected to the topic of discussion. Save those ideas and use them at a later time to expand on the conversation you just had and provide more value to the interaction in general.

Clarify

- something is unclear about the story, be sure to ask questions so that you can get the complete picture. Again, as with reflection, you will not only get all the information, but you will show attentiveness.

Summarize

- the story comes to an end, draw up a quick summary to let the person know you've understood and listened to every they've said and thanked them for the story.

Now there are many types of listening that have been differentiated by science, but for the sake of keeping this to the point, I'm only going to go over two of them, which I believe are crucial for improving your social skills and upgrading on active listening.

The first one of them is sympathetic listening. Sympathy is a term, which is related to the perception, understanding, and caring for a problem or need of another individual. True sympathy cannot be faked under any circumstances, yet it is crucial to developing high-quality relationships. Sympathetic listening expands on the premise of sympathy and transfers it to not only understanding the other person's issues but also acting to help them. If you're hearing a story about how recently a family member deceased, provide the speaker with as much comfort as possible. Show them that they're not alone and possibly, depending on the situation, explain to them that life goes on. Then try to cheer them up by doing something together that they enjoy or maybe just grieving with them. Always try to be perceptive of what the other person needs, in order not to come out as rude or inconsiderate and, in such situations, if something seems out of line, it most probably is, so save it for yourself.

The second type of listening I'm going to discuss is empathetic listening. Empathy is different from sympathy in one key way – when sympathizing with someone you're understanding how they feel and try to make them feel better by taking certain actions. Empathy, on the other hand, is when a true connection and understanding is shared so that you can feel what the other person is feeling and the ability to put yourself in their shoes. You can't feel empathic to strangers, so this is more likely going to reserved for your close friends and family alone. Nevertheless, it's a good idea for you to familiarize yourself with the principles of empathy and why it's so important in establishing quality communication, as it can be a powerful tool to win people over. When showing true empathy to others, we reassure them that we really care about their issues and provide them with the security to open up to us, completely. This not only helps our communication with people but also allows us to achieve a deeper level of connection with each other.

Finally, I would like to give you one more example of poor communication to further illustrate the importance of positive thinking in our interactions with others.

When I was working at the dealership, I already shared the story of how my colleagues became envious of me when I scored the record for the most sales. One of them was particularly jealous. Let's call him John. John came up to me the following day and attempted to make a connection with me, in order to learn some new tactics, I presume. That's perfectly ok with me, since like I said, knowing means nothing if you can't share it with others. So we start talking and as I begin explaining my journey I notice this grin show up on his face. At the time, I thought nothing of it, maybe he had gone through something similar before. I mention my previous job at the printing company and he starts laughing. Naturally, I get confused and I ask him what's so funny about the story. He then proceeds to explain to me how he comes from a wealthy family and has never had to work a single day during his college years. He was trying to shame me for not coming from a wealthy family, which is ridiculous. I just tell him that we all have to start somewhere and that I'm not ashamed of my humble roots. The next day I come into work and I see my colleagues gathered together and laughing at something. I go up to them and am greeted with, "What's up, newspaper boy?". To me, this felt not like a blow like they had assumed it would make me feel, but as a compliment. In their own way, they were congratulating me for achieving what I have achieved by making fun of how hard I've had to work to get to where I am at the moment. Obviously, they didn't think of it this way and continued laughing about it. I was now more motivated than ever. They kept laughing and I kept working as hard as I could. The following month, the dealership's owner comes around and he takes me to his office. He says:

- I see that you're having a hard time fitting in here. Don't pay attention to those unmotivated people that work here. I've seen your results and I'm deeply impressed with what you have achieved. Is there anything that I can do to help you fit in better, if you want to fit in, that is.

- I'm feeling rather fine, thank you. Their petty insults only make me work harder, not to prove to them that I'm wrong, but they serve as motivation for me to one day be able to teach them what I've learned and pass my knowledge on.

- I'm really glad you said that. – he says – I've been thinking about this for a while and I believe now is the right time to do it. My current sales manager at this location has never had results anywhere near close to what you have achieved here, despite being here for such a short time. I'm going to offer you his position. Obviously, it comes with many benefits, including that you get to be their boss and teach them. If you make them do half as well as you have been doing until now, this dealership is going to be the best one in the city. So what do you say?

- That's really kind of you, thank you. But what will happen to the current sales manager?

- He'll be offered your position, if he refuses to take it, well he'll quit. Regardless of whether you accept my offer or not, he's not going to be the sales manager anymore.

- In such case, I feel no guilt in accepting and I look forward to delivering the results that you need.

- Perfect, I'll let them know that they now have a new boss and just watch how their faces change.

I'm not telling this story to brag, but to show you how being positive and staying away from gossip and drama, of course when combined with the proper skills, can pave your way to a better career in no time at all. I may be mistaken, but I believe that if I had involved myself in their petty game and tried to "stick it back to them" I would never have received that promotion in the first place. Furthermore, I went on to develop an astonishing relationship with the dealership's owner, who has helped me numerous times even after I was no longer working for him. The moral of the story is that as long as you stay positive and away from drama, good things will always come your way. Don't forget to educate yourself and stay ahead of the competition.

In the next chapter, we're going to discuss conversations and how to be the best you can be at leading one. I look forward to seeing you there!

ASSET 4 - HOW TO BECOME A BETTER CONVERSATIONALIST

In this chapter, we're going to dissect conversations and delve into the specifics of what makes a person good at holding a conversation. The importance of being skilled at conversations is impossible to understate since after all, social skills are meant to lead to just that – conversations. Before we go into detail about how you can improve your skills, however, I'm going to show you two examples of the same conversation that where being good at conversations can transform the outcome dramatically.

Let's imagine the following scenario: You're out at a bar and want to make a new acquaintance, let's say that's going to be a girl. We're not going to discuss flirting in this chapter, so focus your minds on the things you're about to read.

Conversation 1:

- Hi, my name is Derrek, it's really nice to meet you.
- Hi, Derek, my name is Jean and it's a pleasure to meet you too.
- So… what are you doing here tonight?
- Well, I went out to have a few drinks, take my mind off of work and the other things that are troubling me at the moment.
- Gosh, I feel you. I had the most horrendous week ever. Work was so busy and stressful that I just couldn't wait for the weekend, you know?
- Yeah, same here. So what do you do for work?
- I'm a car salesman, I work at the ABC dealership downtown. Actually, I'm on my way to becoming the sales manager at the moment.
- Wow, good for you, Derrek.
- Yeah, I've put in a lot of work and I believe I've earned this promotion. It's going to come with a big paycheck, too!

- Great. Hey, listen, I don't mean to be rude, but I really would rather be alone with my thoughts at the moment. Catch you later.
- Yeah, bye.

This situation probably looks familiar to some of you. Can you spot what's wrong with this conversation? Try to think of the last time you spoke to a stranger at a social place, such as a bar, and remember the conversation that you had. Was it any similar to this one? I've noticed that people oftentimes don't realize their own mistakes until they see them highlighted as I've done here, so before you keep reading, try to identify where I went wrong and this imaginative conversation and why Jean walked away?

Have you figured out the reasons yet? So what my figurative me did in this conversation is to make a few key errors.

Mistake number one: The follow – up

So let's say you've mustered up the courage to go and talk to a stranger at a bar, an introduction is a great way to start the ball rolling. However, directly after the introduction is where mistake number one was made. Although it is correct to ask the other person a question, you have to make that question personal. "What are you doing here tonight" sounds like "You don't look like the type of person that goes to (insert venue) and I really think that you don't fit in with the environment". In case the person you were talking to was less agreeable than our imaginary Jean, you would've been cut off right there and then. Instead, what you should follow up with is a personal question, possibly preceded by a compliment. We're going to take a look at an example conversation with corrections after we discuss all the mistakes made.

Mistake number two: Switching the focus to yourself

When you're the one approaching somebody and initializing the conversation, it's rather obvious that you're the one who's showing interest. It's ok to throw in a few details about yourself, after all, this is a conversation, not an interrogation, but you have to keep the focus on them. This subconsciously signals the other person that you're genuinely interested in what they have to say and makes them engage in the conversation more actively. Of course, if they ask you a question back, answer that question with a reasonable amount of detail – not in one word, but also don't go on explaining how you got your job after 10+ years of training, etc.

Mistake number three: Complaining

Did you notice the difference between the way Jean expressed that she had a rough week and how my imaginary me did it? It's ok to say "I have to take my mind off of something", it's not ok to complain. Why? Think about it – would you feel good if someone came up to you to complain? Would you want to continue that conversation and, possibly, meet up another time with that person? I didn't think so, therefore you should avoid complaining as much as possible, regardless of the hardships that you have to go through on a daily basis. We all do, but keep them to yourself.

Mistake number four: Bragging

When Jean asked about my profession, I went on to explain that, currently, I work as a sales agent, but I would soon be a sales manager, which would come with a great paycheck increase. Why would that be ok to say to someone you've known for 2 minutes? It isn't. It's not going to give much information to anybody and, the most it could do is attract a potential gold digger. Never flaunt wealth, career or other achievements this early on. It makes you look cocky and self-centered and nobody likes being friends with those people.

Mistake number five: Letting them go

We've all heard this before – if you love someone let them go and if they come back they love you too. This doesn't work for this type of situation. There is no love involved. If you've stepped out of line or bored the other person, it's not too late to apologize and start over. If anything, it might even increase your chances of getting a quality conversation, because now you know what topics to avoid with that person.

So after discussing these mistakes, let's resume from where we left off

- Great. Hey, listen, I don't mean to be rude, but I really would rather be alone with my thoughts at the moment. Catch you later.
- I'm sorry, Jean, I get like that sometimes. If you don't mind me asking, what do you do for work?
- I thought you'd never ask. Well, I'm an (insert profession)
- Wow, that's amazing. You know, as a kid I dreamt of being an (insert profession)
- Really? No way!
- Yeah, I did. Why did you decide to become an (insert profession)
- Well, it's been a passion of mine since I was a child. I've always wanted to do this. Why did you become a car salesman?
- It's actually a really long story that I'd rather not get into now, but let's just say I had to improve my people skills and I decided to dive headfirst.(answer the question without going into

too much detail but still provide a decent enough answer.)

- Wow, that's really cool. I wish I had the courage to do something like that

- I bet you do, in fact, I'm going to challenge you to show you that you do!

- No, no, I really can't do it.

- Yes, you can. Ok, here's the challenge. I want you to go up to that table over there with your drink and say: "Hey, guys, I'm really sorry for interrupting you, I just wanted to say cheers." (Break the stereotype. Think of something simple to challenge them with what can be done with little to no effort and risk. This will break the ice even further and will show the other person that you're open to experimenting and dealing with odd situations)

- Oh, god, alright.

- Jean comes back, you chat some more. It's getting late and you have to leave.

- Jean, it's been a real pleasure meeting you tonight. I would like to invite you to hang out sometime again. Maybe we could exchange numbers?

(Don't ask a question at this point such as would you like to hang out with me. That leaves them the option to say no. Instead, say that you'd really enjoy going out with them again and offer a way of setting it up)

- You know what, Derrek, you were off to a pretty bad start, but I actually like you too. Here's my number, call me next Friday and we'll think of something.

- Done deal. Until next Friday!

So as you can see, the conversation went in a drastically different way by adjusting just a few things in my hypothetical behavior. There are a few more do's and don'ts in conversation etiquette, which we are going to list below, but keep in mind that as long as you stay receptive and try to perceive what the other person may be feeling about the topics of discussion, you could really make a difference in their life, as well as your own.

I'd like to start with the don'ts here, because I often observe people communicating in their own manner, which usually contains a mixture of good and bad techniques and I believe that learning what to avoid is more important than learning what to do, when it comes to a skill as natural to us as speaking, that is.

Number one: NEVER interrupt

This should come at no surprise to anyone, but interrupting someone during a conversation is a sign of disrespect and will definitely be noticed by the other person/people. Some of the other don'ts are more subtle, but when you interrupt someone speaking, you risk terminating the conversation altogether.

Number 2: Don't try to come out on top.

This is something that I see happening all the time, mostly when a group has formed by primarily same-sex individuals. What happens is someone opens a topic – let's say cars – and they each go on to explain what car they got, how much money they spent on it and whatnot. Although this is mostly typical for younger people, I've seen people over 40 do it as well. Fighting for dominance does nobody any good and wastes everybody's time. If you are forced into a situation like this, try to change the topic or just avoid this part of the conversation at all.

Number 3: Don't ever ask if you're boring somebody

If you have to ask, chances are you are. Even if you weren't, the fact that you thought you might be will make you boring to them. If you find yourself in a situation where you're really urging to ask that, just change the topic or look for body language cues to give you the answer you were so desperately seeking.

Do's:

Number 1: Always be polite and respectful

I believe that this should apply to every type of communication, regardless of whether you've just met the person or you've known them for 20 years. Politeness is crucial, especially with new contacts and will let the other person know that you mean them no wrong. Being respectful on the other hand will earn you respect as well since most people believe that respect is given in equal measure to the respect received.

Number 2: Be yourself

It's fairly transparent to others when you're forcing yourself into saying things that you normally wouldn't. Just be yourself and people will like you for who you are. This brings the added benefit of not having to maintain an image in case someone likes the "fake" you, which you presented to them. Believe me, this can turn into a nightmare in the blink of an eye.

Number 3: Always tell the truth

Lying and all attempts of deception are generally a poor way of making new friends. Telling the truth, however, can go a really long way with pretty much everyone. Did you screw up by being late? Don't make up some bull-shit excuse, just say what really happened. You once had

25 cars parked in front of your house? Of course, you didn't, just tell the truth and no one will go looking for that perfect lie of yours.

This concludes the chapter on conversations. Once again, if you are in doubt whether something is appropriate – it most probably isn't and you should keep it to yourself. Follow the tips and conversation examples above and you'll be the master of conversation in no time. If you want to practice the conversation scenarios as we did here, you could ask a friend of yours to sit down with you and pretend you were just meeting and play out different scenarios. Of course, you would have to instruct them to act as if they were just meeting you and to try to be as real as possible. This can save you some trial and error with strangers or people that you aren't really comfortable with. You could also ask them to highlight any errors that you're making in your conversations. Best of luck and I'll see you in the next chapter, where we'll be discussing body language! Ooh, this is exciting!

ASSET 5 – YOUR BODY LANGUAGE SAYS A LOT ABOUT YOU

Body language has to be one of my favorite topics to discuss with people, mostly because it's so largely underestimated, yet learning how to control these subconscious cues can have the most tremendous effects on your communication. Wait, subconscious? That was something to do with psychology, right? You are correct, in psychology, the term subconscious refers to the part of our conscience that isn't currently focal. However, the subconscious is crucial to communication, since it can be responsible for interpreting up to 90% of all incoming signals. Have you ever wondered why you get a feeling that someone isn't interested in the conversation that you're having at the moment or that they're generally not into you? That's your subconscious speaking, telling you that it has registered some of the other person's non-verbal cues and flagged them as alarming. Well, these non-verbal cues are out of their control, right? Wrong, non-verbal cues can very much be controlled, although it requires a significant amount of attention and training. Reading those cues, however, is rather simpler and more easily achievable. In this chapter, we're going to discuss some of the most important non-verbal cues that you can give off and read in others, known as body language. Body language refers to the conveying of information via body movements, posture, gestures and pretty much everything that you can do with your body, both consciously and unconsciously. I won't lie to you, body language is a pretty complicated matter, but then again, if you really want to improve your social skills, learning the basics of this is rather important.

Before we go any further, I would like to point out a few important things about body language in general. It can often be tempting to draw conclusions based on just one of the factors that we're about to discuss, but you should keep in mind that in order for one to properly make deductions based on body language, they need to have the complete picture. You may have heard some clichés before, such as that if a person has their arms crossed they really aren't receptive to what you're saying and are generally blocking you out. That is true, but only if matched with other body language cues. I, for example, tend to cross my arms during certain conversations, not because I'm not receptive, but because if I'm standing up I find it odd to just let my arms hang. You must always assume that the person may just be comfortable in this position and not be doing it in an attempt to convey any information at all. Therefore, a complete analysis of one's body language must be done before any accurate conclusions can be drawn. Please, be aware that underestimating this aspect of body language may lead to many misunderstandings and even more adverse situations, such as entering an argument with somebody.

To illustrate the importance of body language, I'd like to present two different scenarios, in which only body language will change. The situation will be identical to the one we discussed in the previous chapter. My imaginary self is in a bar meeting Jean for a follow-up for a second encounter. This time, we've already established that we're mutually interested in one another, however, my imaginary self has some making up to do. As you remember, in the previous chapter Jean and I didn't get off on the right foot. So it's time we make things up, right?

Jean and I have agreed to meet up in a different bar downtown. After all, this isn't a date, not yet, so we don't want things to become too intimate by going to a restaurant together. Don't worry, we will get to dating in one of the next chapters, be patient and learn from what you're about to read. We meet up at the agreed time, sit at the bar and grab a drink each. We start talking about more intimate matters, such as family, personal interests, hobbies, friends, etc. while remembering to follow the proper rules of communication we discussed earlier. Everything seems to be going rather well until Jean ask a rather weird question:

- Am I intimidating you?
- Haha, no, why would you ask that?
- Well, I don't really know, I just get the general feeling that you're not feeling too comfortable.

You see, Jean had picked up on some of the unconscious cues I had been giving away this whole time. When looking at a person's body language, here are some telltale signs that they're not feeling particularly comfortable. I had gradually, over the course of the conversation, moved further away from her, initially pulling to the backside of my chair, then moving my chair back a bit. Creating distance between two people suggests that you aren't feeling too comfortable with them being close and gives away signs of insecurity. Furthermore, I had started facing towards the bar, rather than to Jean and I would only turn my head to her when talking to her. Keep an eye on people's posture when talking to them. If their feet are pointed away from you, that means that they're starting to feel a bit uncomfortable and are subconsciously looking for an exit. If their entire body is turned away from you, this is a surefire way of knowing that they're going into defense mode. Usually, this behavior will be accompanied by a noticeable decrease in answer length. So when you ask a question, they will answer as briefly as possible, shifting the spotlight back to you. This can mean a few things; they either feel insecure or they're really not interested in the conversation. Possibly the most important single factor that you need to be on the lookout for is synchrony. Synchrony can tell you how much on the same page you and the other person really are. It's exceptionally important when the encounter is somewhat romantic or with one single person. Synchrony is expressed by syncing one's body language cues with the other person's. You can test synchrony by deliberately changing your posture and observing their response. If they match it with yours quickly, then you are most likely on the same page.

Although, it can be rather difficult to properly illustrate a proper example of body language in a person who is comfortable and relaxed without going into J.R.R. Tolkien style, here are some other cues that you can be looking out for.

- Eye contact is largely culture-specific, you can assume that if someone is maintaining eye contact with you and not deliberately avoiding it, they are being honest and sincere with you. Furthermore, we've all heard that eye is a window to the soul and that is absolutely true. Our eyes are the only part of body language that cannot be deliberately manipulated. Avoiding eye contact and looking around the room is generally an expression of lack of interest and seeking an escape of some sort.

- The handshake can be crucial to how an interaction begins. It is the first point of contact between people, thus it tells us what the other person has in mind. There are a few points of interest in a handshake. To start with, palm contact is crucial. If the other person deliberately tries to keep his palm from yours, it can be identified as withholding some information back from you or having the intention to be deceitful in the following communication. If the handshake is too firm it's a sign of anxiety and/or fear. If you notice the other person trying to twist their arm to be on top of yours, that is an attempt to demonstrate dominance over you and "establish" themselves as the dominant one in the interaction.

- There are also plenty of genders and person-specific body language cues that you should be on the lookout for, which can generally be recognized by observing the same movement in certain situations, much like a poker "tell". Certain people will use those when lying to disguise the lie or when signaling that they are attracted to you as a sign of nervousness. Although they can vary vastly between individuals, once you learn to recognize these "tells" you will know that pretty much everyone has one. Some women flick their hair back, some guys tap their foot, they can really be anything. Be observant and you'll notice them right away.

At this point, you may be asking yourself why is all that information important? Wasn't this book supposed to be about improving my social skills, not about body language? You couldn't be further from the truth, though. You see, social skills that you can use are only a part of the complete package. In order to become truly masterful at communication, you need to be able to fully understand the other person and all the information that they may be trying to communicate to you. This is where body language shines – when properly interpreted, these non-verbal cues can help you identify what the other person is really trying to say, even if they can't or won't say it out loud. Furthermore, learning to control your body language can help you control the information that you're giving others or, more likely, control the information that you don't want to give away. This is especially important in the business world, where a single missed cue or one interpreted the wrong way can make or break your deals. High-level businessmen study body language in-depth in order to have a competitive edge over those below them in the hierarchy. You may not be a high-level businessman, but you can certainly use the same practices that they do to improve your business, regardless of whether you actually own one or you work for one. The next time you walk into your boss's office with a brilliant idea and you have learned body language you are much more likely to receive permission to act on it. Maybe even a promotion after that, who knows. The point is that the better you are to become at the art of body language, the more opportunities will come knocking on your doorstep, just waiting for you to take them.

Although body language is a field of study in its own right and it's mostly used to interpret other people's cues on a conscious level, compared to the typical subconscious evaluation, there are certain steps that you can take to avoid sending out the wrong message to others.

1. Be aware – although this is something I keep coming back to, I really can't stress enough how important it is. Being aware will always help you with your communication with others, regardless of the level that you're having that communication at. Furthermore, in this particular case, it will provide more efficient readings of the other person's body language specifics.

2. We talked about mirroring as a cue that you can use to see if the other person is on the same page as you, however, mirroring can also be used when

listening to someone speak. By mirroring their body language, even subtly, you will create synergy and help the conversation flow easier, by putting them at ease and showing them that you care.

3. Always be as relaxed as possible – tension can be passed on from one person to the next, so if you are feeling tense you are very likely to transfer that to your conversation partner, which can by no means be good for the flow of the interaction.

4. Face the other person – once again, even though we discussed this earlier as something to be on the lookout for, facing your conversation partner will result in a more substantial connection and better interactions in general.

5. Mind how you're crossing your arms and legs – although it can feel comfortable like it feels for me, it can send off the wrong message to those that don't know better than to judge by one cue alone. If you notice that your partner is giving you a look when you cross your arms or legs, simply

undo it and you will be in the clear. Furthermore, it can be easing for you and them.

By now, it should be becoming clear to you that each of these chapters is as important as the other ones and that in order for you to be great at social interaction, you need master each of these aspects and practice them. Body language is absolutely no different than the others, however, it can be more important than some. Unfortunately, diving deeply in the specifics of body language would defeat the purpose of this book, but perhaps we'll make an entire one specifically on it. In the meantime, though, feel free to explore other sources of information on body language and practice everything that you learn. In the next chapter, we're going to look at various ways of meeting new people, I look forward to seeing you there.

ASSET 6 – MEETING NEW PEOPLE

I hope you have been keeping up on your practice from the previous chapters because it's about to get real. We're about to dive into the specifics of how to actually apply the principles we've discussed in the previous chapters in real life. In this chapter, we're going to talk about meeting new people through various different channels and how to actually create relationships out of those encounters. Without further due, let's begin:

The Introduction

Now, this should go without saying, but introducing yourself is the most important part of creating new relationships, bar none. Why is that? Well, it's simple – people trust their gut instincts a lot and their first impression of you is very likely to remain unchanged if it's a bad one. It is possible for you to turn the table on yourself and change a good first impression to a bad one as time goes on, but believe me, if someone gets a negative impression about you the first time they meet you – they'll do everything in their power to limit further communication with you. You would do the same, right? How is a first impression created then? Well, I'm glad you asked. For the most part, the first impression is based on your body language, clothing, cleanliness, and manners. We've discussed body language in the previous chapter, clothes, and cleanliness. So is this chapter going to be about my manners, then? No, it's going to be about how you actually make someone get a first impression of you. You have to introduce yourself properly, this is absolutely vital, especially in today's world. With communications available across all sorts of different platforms and media, it can exceptionally hard to get someone's attention and in a way "force" them to have a conversation with you. Furthermore, it's actually very difficult to approach someone and not come across as 'creepy' to them. After all, wouldn't you be a bit freaked out if someone came up to you and asked for your name?

I would. The odds are stacked against you, against everyone. Although I would love to go into a deep thought train about why this happens, this is not the point. Before you actually introduce yourself to somebody, you have to make sure they are receptive to an introduction. If you're at a social place, such as a bar or a café, look for people that aren't on their smartphones or whatever other device they may be carrying. They are absorbed in their own current reality and you pulling them away from it is not a good start, at all. Then, use the body language tips from the previous chapter to try and determine what the person is thinking about if they're relaxed or tense about something. In essence, you're trying to sift out the people that you will be welcomed by from those that will immediately reject your approach. Although it is possible for someone to just be on their phone out of boredom and your entrance to be accepted with an open mind, I find that it's better if you avoid potential disasters and stick to the guidelines above.

Now that you know whom to approach, it's time to make an entrance. Now, there are numerous variables that might alter the way you should introduce yourself and even more people saying that they've found the "secret" to a great start. I, on the other hand, like keeping things simple. My go-to introduction for most scenarios is a simple: "Hi, my name is Derrek.". Now obviously, in a formal scenario, you would opt for hello, instead of hi and also include your last name, as well as your first. Depending on the setting of the encounter, I like adding a touch that will "break the ice", for example, if I'm at a bar and I'm approaching someone – I'll ask what it is that they're drinking or toss in a compliment about their choice of drink. Don't go overboard at this stage by saying something along the lines of, "I saw you from across the room, you're really beautiful", that would just make you look like a creep and nobody likes those guys. Be gentle at the start, after all, you're the one showing interest and taking the other person away from what they're doing. Ideally, this is the part where you learn the other person's name, which opens up the next opportunity to screw it all up. We've all been in the situation where we meet someone new, they introduce themselves to us and immediately after we've forgotten their name. It's not a pleasant scenario and this is how you avoid it – as soon as you learn their name, use it when asking your next question. This will not only help you remember their name but will show them that you're listening to what they're saying and taking it to a personal level. Once you've got the hang of that, the rest is in your hands. As a rule of thumb, I like to begin the conversation around something that we're both mutually interested in and if I don't know what the other person is interested in, I gather that information by starting a discussion about the place that we've met and/or the experience surrounding it. In doing so, I guide the other speaker to reveal themselves to be a bit more and give me something to hold on to when taking the conversation to a more personal level. If you happen to know this person's background (for example, they said that they do this and that for work) you could take the conversation in that direction, but you should always be mindful of the environment, because they may be in that particular place by themselves to avoid thinking and/or talking about work. Be creative when trying to break the ice, it can't hurt anybody. This is also a good time to throw in a few jokes, but keep them non-offensive at all costs.

If we're taking things to a professional environment, I find that, much like in business, the introduction is a value proposition. Keep it short and to the point. Here's what that might look like:

- my name is (your name) and I'm an (insert profession). I currently work for (company) and this is what I do for them:_____. I've been with them for this many years and am currently responsible for (insert) aspects of the business. It's a pleasure to meet you.

- Of course, you would have to fill these out for yourself, but I find that by introducing yourself in a similar way you create pull towards you and immediately tell people who you are, what you do and how you can be useful for them or they for you.

- I have a personal preference for bars, cafés, and other public gathering places, not everyone does. They come with many advantages, such as the mood being set by the place, the fact that people go there to relax and many more, but they also have many disadvantages. Perhaps the most crucial one is that the chances for you to meet someone with similar interests to yours are next to none unless your main interest is visiting such locations, that is. After all, those are rather neutral places where people from different backgrounds and with vastly different interests tend to go. In order to find people that are more likely to be similar to you in one way or another, here are some alternative ways to meet new people, which can speed up the process of acquiring new friends and possibly improve the quality of the relationships.

- My absolute favorites are hobby classes. They're amazing, especially if you're taking a beginner's class. For example, when I was in college and struggling to find peers of my own, I decided to sign up for a locksmithing class. I was very shy at the time and dancing or other social activities were a nightmare for me, so locksmithing it was. I thought it was just going to be me and the instructor, but I was surprised to find about 15 people in that class. Over the next four months, two of them became my friends and we still hang out to this day, although not nearly as frequently. Hobby classes provide a semi-neutral environment, because you're not at your home or the other person's home, yet you know their name since you probably were introduced to one another by the instructor and you immediately have a topic for discussion. They take a lot of the guesswork away from what is otherwise a rather painstaking process, especially if you're not comfortable around strangers. Sign up for one and you won't regret it.

- The next thing that I like to do when trying to meet new people is to sign up for any sort of group activity, based on what I'm into at the moment. Whether it's a book group, a debate meeting or even profession-specific groups, these can be another way to finely tune your compass for new contacts. Furthermore, these groups usually bring value to you, whether it's in improving your skills or providing you with brainstorming partners, there's a lot to be had there.

- you are willing to explore the avenue of getting to know people from your workplace or field better, or in other words, you don't hate their guts, here are some tips to help you with that:

1. If you work in an office, use lunchtime to socialize. Don't get on your phone, pretending to work or be busy, but go out and talk to your colleagues. You'll most probably find that at least one of them is actually a really cool person and you will wish you had made this change sooner.

2. Don't skip after-work group activities. Sometimes, colleagues will propose a night out on Fridays or a barbeque at someone's house on Sunday. You get the idea, usually, there are plenty

of opportunities to socialize, because they, just like you, are looking for that extra communication and are struggling to find it elsewhere.

3. Don't skip teambuilding exercises. Teambuilding exercises function as a group class, in my opinion. You all know each other by name, but you're stuck in an activity of some sort for a given period of time and you might as well make the most of it. Use these opportunities to show your colleagues your off-work side and experience something new with them.

Now, here's an opportunity for you to use social media to your advantage. I've pointed out that social media is, in my opinion, a bigger problem than it is a solution, but you can actually use it for some beneficial things as well. When meeting people through social media you have to keep a few things in mind. First off, I would avoid approaching strangers on social media in a 1 on 1 setting, such as a private message. This is creepy and even if you don't come off as creepy, you will look desperate.

Instead, try finding groups about activities/topics that you like and enjoy and become active on them. Regardless of the media that you choose to use, there are plenty of options on every one of them. Once you've been active for a while you will probably notice other active members as well and chances are they'll notice you too. This might be a good time to introduce yourself, using the tips we discussed above and if the group is local, maybe even set up a meeting with them. Often times, groups that revolve around activities, such as biking, hiking, dog walking or whatever else it may be, will host regular events for their members and will offer an opportunity for you to meet the people you've been talking to in real life, without having to go through the trouble of messaging them and setting up a meeting. There are also certain apps that are specifically targeted at local residents and the activities that they like, which can be a huge help on the quest to find new friends. However, as this is an online-only experience, I would advise you to remain cautious about potential cat-fishers. I was once almost caught in a cat-fishing situation with an ex-girlfriend of mine, which wasn't a pleasant experience at all. She was posing as someone else on social media and trying to get my interest and specifically insisting that we meet as soon as possible, which sounded fishy to me at first. She then gave herself away by using a very specific phrase that instantly reminded me of her and I confronted her about it. However, I was lucky that the person trying to cat-fish me was someone that I knew well. Be careful out there and be even more careful as we're entering the next chapter, where we'll be discussing dating – the most statistically likely reason that you're reading this book in general.

ASSET 7 – THE DREADED ONE: DATING

I've been where you are, believe me. I failed at a relationship after relationship until things became unbearable. I had to trace my steps back and find the reason for this madness that was going on in my dating life. I couldn't possibly be so bad at dating, could I? Well, I could and I was, so I did trace my steps back to my very first relationship. I was just a kid in high school when love struck me for the first time. At least I thought so at the time. Her name was Ashley and she was the queen of my heart, that's what I used to call her. She was pretty, smart and liked the same things that I did – what more could a man want from a woman? Our relationship started off as a friendship, which gradually over the course of two years transformed into a relationship, sort of. You see, there are no classes on dating in high school.

Nor are there any on how to behave in a relationship - what is acceptable and what isn't - how to set certain rules about the relationship in general so I knew absolutely nothing about this. Neither did she. So we did what everyone else was doing – we adopted a certain model of a relationship from our parents that we've seen for years and maybe even some of their habits, such as calling each other honey, love, pumpkin, etc. The problem is that the modern child is born relatively late in their parents' lives when compared to say, 100 years ago and they've missed the opportunity to learn about the different phases of a relationship from their parents and jump straight into the mid 30's married couple that has a steady job, an already well-established routine and generally, they have it all figured out. I was no different and together with Ashley made all the mistakes we possibly could. For the better part of two years, we would suffocate each other, not allowing any room for individual activities, we would spend all of our time together, down to the last minute of it, robbing us of the opportunity to interact and become closer to other people, we were so jealous of each other that we would even go to the extremes of not wanting to sleep apart for more than one night. As you can imagine, this caused its fair share of problems for the two of us. Although our education didn't suffer, our personal relationships with everyone else did, majorly. I remember being so devoted to this girl that I would ignore my best friend at the time, whom I eventually lost. And all of a sudden, high school was over and she was headed off to college in a different state. Disaster struck for both of us. We hadn't spent more than a day without one another for the past two years. Luckily for us, we made the smart decision and agreed to go our separate ways and not try to maintain a long-distance relationship throughout college. However, what came next was completely devastating – how was I supposed to learn to live without her? Meet other people? I realized that I had no friends, no groups of people to hang out with – nothing. I was all alone. And then it struck me – I had done everything wrong. I can imagine that the situation was identical for Ashley because we would talk to each other frequently after we separated, and she was experiencing the same troubles I was. So what did go wrong? Why did we fail so miserably at the game of dating? We'll get to that in a bit, but first, let's switch back to you and how you should approach dating to begin with.

As I mentioned previously, it is my firm belief that the lack of education on romantic relationships is detrimental to modern society more than it has ever been before. We're stuck in a loop where the information we have on dating comes from our peers who are dating, but who are also as clueless as we are about what dating is supposed to look like. Not to mention that one single failed relationship at an early stage in your life can set you back tremendously as it did with me. So how do you break free from this cycle? By learning, but it's hard to learn when no one is prepared to give you the information and you're probably too shy to ask anyway. I'm not going to go into detail about how you should score yourself a date, mostly because this is a very controversial topic and many other professionals have already expressed their opinion on the topic. What I will say is that as long as you stick to the social rules and brush up on your social skills, you are very likely to get a date with the person that you want. The one tip that I will give you in this department is to be confident and go after what you want. Confidence beats almost every other quality at the early stages of getting to know someone and showing your romantic interest in them. Be brave and pursue that pretty guy/girl that you met last week and show them that you're interested, tell them that you like them and take things from there. Don't get caught in the cycle of hanging out constantly but never having your relationship evolve in any way.

So once you get to dating, there are many things we need to talk about.

I would like to begin by stating the importance of compromise. I've been in a relationship for about 10 years now and believe me, compromise is key. You won't have everything go exactly the way you planned it to, there will be some things that you will have to miss out on, but you will have a healthy relationship in which both you and your partner feel happy. Don't obsess over small details, such as the place you'll go out to next Friday if your date has a strong opinion on that. In general, avoid getting into unnecessary conflict by saying you won't do something, just because you want to be the decision-maker. That doesn't mean that you should always agree to whatever your partner is saying, but rather that it's ok to go out for pizza tonight, even though you kind of wanted to get Chinese, but your partner really loves pizza and well, you do too.

Next in terms of importance comes stimulation. Compromise will mostly be used in relationships that you've already established are worthy of your time, stimulation, on the other hand, will help you sift out potential good partners from potential bad partners. I see this all the time, especially in younger people, who spend months and years together, simply because they're afraid of being alone. They're not really in love with their partner, they're not really happy with them either, but it's better than nothing, right? Wrong. When choosing how far you're willing to go with someone, I suggest using the method of stimulation. Think about your interactions with that person and how stimulating they are to you. Do you think of them and the things you talked about on the next day? Do you go out of your way to learn something new so that you're better prepared to discuss with them the next time you get the chance? You get the idea. In their essence, relationships are contracts that people make voluntarily. You agree to spend your time and energy with someone, in exchange for their time and energy, but also the positive experiences and knowledge that you gain in the process. After all, you wouldn't spend $100 on a course in finances from your neighbor Billy, who's broke and has $20k debt, would you? Of course not, what does Billy know about finances? So why would you invest your time and energy into a relationship that isn't going to be beneficial to you, even if it ends at some point in time? You wouldn't if you could think rationally about dating, but that's not always the case, which brings me to my next point.

Ditch the perfect world glasses

It's often tempting to just let yourself flow over the course of a relationship, thinking that everything is normal, because hey, no relationship is perfect. While that is true, it doesn't mean that you should conform to society's standards about what's normal and stay in a relationship because of them. If society says beating your spouse is ok, would you be ok with being beaten? Of course not, so why would you be ok with your partner draining life from you? I believe that it's crucial for us as humans to take the time every once in a while to step back and evaluate how our relationship has been progressing until this point, according to our own values. I can't tell you what's right and what's wrong in this particular scenario, because each person's values are different and you have to make that assessment for yourself. Just promise me you will, I just can't stand looking at miserable couples anymore.

Learn from your mistakes

I've often heard the phrase "People learn from their mistakes and smart people learn from the mistakes of others" but it doesn't apply to this case. Dating is very individualistic and you will have to learn from your own mistakes. What I like to do is after a relationship has finished, take some time to be single, evaluate what went wrong and what went right. Possibly adjust the idea of the person that you're looking for to have a relationship with next. Try to find the mistakes not only in your partner but in yourself, so that you can be better for your next partner as well. This is one of those self-reflection practices that I believe can solve many of the world's problems if only everyone applied it. Don't be caught making the same mistake twice, evaluate and then move on.

It's ok to be single

Now, this is a bit of a problem for some people, but you really must learn to be single and to enjoy being single if you want to have a successful relationship with somebody at some point in your life. You can't expect a person to just show up and make you happy, you have to be happy by yourself in order to share your happiness with your partner in a relationship. If you expect happiness to come from someone else, you will most likely never find it. This is why I like to take at least 2 months being single after a break-up before I dive into my next relationship. This is mostly true for longer-term relationships, rather than short flings that don't last, but I'm not trying to teach you how to be a jock, but how to be a true partner here, so take your time.

Perhaps the most important thing I have to say in this chapter is that you should absolutely always speak the truth. Regardless of the situation, the possible outcome or anything else for that matter, being truthful to your partner is a must if you want to build a relationship that will last. Lying is a practice for the weak-minded people who just can't face the consequences of their own actions. If you've screwed up, admit to it and apologize. If your partner is doing something you're not really into – say so, you have the right to have preferences. In general, you won't believe how many times telling the truth will actually earn you respect and the mistake you made may even be overlooked, whereas if your partner found out in some different way, boy are you in trouble.

Always be sure to compliment the other person – we can all use some positive reinforcement.

This should really go without saying, but it's often neglected by many. Tell your partner that they're beautiful, that they have an amazing personality, you can really use anything that you find attractive and great about them. Believe me, when I say, no amount of complimenting is ever too much, but neglect to let the other person know how you feel about them and you'll find them drifting away from you.

Always, and I mean always, *be yourself*

It's rather easy to transform yourself into somebody else for a period of time if you're trying to make an impression of some sort. But when that image has to maintained over a prolonged period of time – not so easy. So why would you even bother doing it in the first place? Stick to who you are and the right people will find you attractive and worthy of their love and you won't have to keep up appearances for a single day in your life.

Social media dating

I feel like I have to touch on this as well, despite the fact I'm strongly against it. Social media dating takes the human element out of the equation. We are presented with an image of someone with a list of their character traits and whatever they've written in their mini biography. It's absurd to me that people actually enjoy swiping through pictures of other people as if they're in the supermarket choosing what to eat for the next week. However, if dating apps are your thing, go for them, use the tips in the chapter on meeting new people to design a proper bio for yourself, sort of like an introduction and be sure to highlight the good parts of your character, but don't exaggerate. Nobody likes a fake.

Let's get back to that story of my failed relationship I was telling you at the beginning of this chapter. Why did it fail?

The reasons are rather simple to me now, but they were incomprehensible to my 18-year-old self. I would like to turn your attention to what I'm about to say because the key to having a successful relationship is understanding what you can expect from one and what to avoid.

A relationship is a safe haven, it's comfort, it's love and it's a passion for each other. What it's not is obsession, lack of personal space, paranoia, and jealousy. When we're children we can't really tell the difference between the two states of a relationship – a healthy and a toxic one. A healthy relationship is one in which both people grow, they learn from each other and are full of love and positive emotions for one another. A toxic one, on the other hand, revolves around trying to take control of the other person, being jealous of their time, their friends and even their family, not striving to grow, but rather to stay where you are now out of fear of losing the relationship.

The issue is that it's often hard to tell a healthy from a toxic relationship because in both cases you're with someone that you love and abuse and jealousy can be justified by love, which is horribly wrong.

In a healthy relationship, each person should have their own time, whether it's to be with friends, family or by themselves and involve themselves in activities that they find interesting. Obviously, each person will have different needs as to the amounts of time, but such a time is a must. We all have hobbies and friends, which aren't particularly interesting to our partners, and that's ok. We just need to have the time for them.

A healthy relationship is one where responsibilities are shared. Regardless of whether you live in one home or not, we all have responsibilities we need to take care of. In order for a relationship to function properly, responsibility must be shared between the two people. It might be something as simple as household chores, which society has deemed "women's work" in the past, but in modern society, where the woman is working just as much as the man is, it's imperative that such mundane activities be shared between the partners.

The partners in a functioning relationship are equal and their contribution to the relationship is also equal. You must understand that relationships are a unit, just like a family, and balance must be kept in them. Have faith in your partner, be truthful to them and your relationship will prosper.

Toxic relationships, on the other hand, are like a plague. They poison us slowly each day, making us resent our partners more and more, despite the fact we love them.

They become unbearable at some point and usually, the break-ups are rough and full of sadness. In some extreme cases, violence is present throughout the relationship as a sign of "love". To understand if your relationship is toxic, you can look at these factors and ask yourself if any of them is present in your relationship.

1. ***Excessive jealousy*** – getting a little jealous if you bump into your partner's ex-partner is human. Being jealous of their time, constantly asking where they are and who they're with is not.

2. ***Abuse*** – abuse comes in many forms and can be disguised as deep love by some manipulative individuals. However, being told what to do, when to do it and being made to feel guilty if you refuse to do so is not something you should tolerate.

3. ***Compulsive behavior and anger*** – if your partner has phases that revolve around them being extremely happy to see you or extremely annoyed at you and get angry at you for no logical

reason, this is a clear sign that your relationship is toxic and you need to move on.

Remember that girl I was telling you about in the earlier chapters that eventually became my wife? I'd like to illustrate that relationships can also be amazing, even more so than they can be terrifying. Last time I wrote about her, she called me back after I dropped the flowers off at her office. We set up a "date", because it really wasn't one. I wanted to get to know this person and understand why she had this pull on me and it was so strong that I could barely focus on anything else. We met up in a coffee shop this time, instead of a bar, so there would be no alcohol intervening with our communication. We spoke for hours about all the different aspects of our lives and had a really positive vibe about one another throughout the whole time. We then started set up a proper date this time, dinner, at a rather unexpected location – a Chinese restaurant. I had proposed to take her to one of the more fashionable places, but she insisted on Chinese, her argument being that she didn't want our financial situations to influence our perception of each other. This I believe is especially important today, when the "Gold Digging" trend is all over the place. You see countless videos on Facebook about someone pranking a gold digger or how someone is a gold digger, etc. When dating someone that you haven't known for a long time, steer clear of expensive options for dates or gifts. Not because they don't deserve them or they might prove to be a gold digger, but because you wouldn't want your financial situation to influence their perception of you as a person, regardless of whether in a positive or a negative way. Society focusses too much on money and material possessions, while overlooking personality traits, that are crucial to a successful relationship. Which is, in my opinion, the reason why my relationship with Gwen developed so splendidly afterwards. We each had our own goals and ambitions in life, however, we never let money or any material possessions affect how we felt about each other. Other people were buying houses and expensive cars at the time when we were striving to build our businesses and well, today we're in a pretty good place, both financially and emotionally. What I'm trying to say is that you should always value the other person for everything else, except money, and you will have a much clearer understanding of whether you are compatible or not, thus making your relationship healthier.

This concludes this chapter of the book, I wish to once again urge you to be kind, compassionate and loving to your partners if creating a long-term relationship is what you're after. Follow these tips on building a relationship and you'll be on your way to that sweet family life in no time.

ASSET 8 – STRENGTHENING FRIENDSHIPS AND BUILDING CONNECTIONS

The most important reason for developing your socials skills are connections with other people. Simply put, this is the ultimate reason why anyone would do anything in life at all. Humans are known as "social animals", which means that we cannot exist as an individual, we always become part of some sort of a tribe. Whether this tribe is work-related or hobby-related. Whether it's a family or a circle of friends, we've practiced being a part of a group since the beginning of the human race. Initially, being part of a group was a necessity for survival, we simply weren't on the top of the food-chain with many more powerful and bigger animals roaming the Earth. A tribe nowadays is not necessary for our most basic survival needs, such as food and water, mostly thanks to the invention of the trading of goods, but that does not mean that the human race hasn't changed at all since the old times. We've evolved to be able to provide food through trade, water is readily available in most countries and our basic needs are covered. However, a study conducted in 2013 suggests that humans, in general, have a built-in need to speak, not to themselves, that is. Why is this important? Well, human communication has been studied by numerous scientists in a number of different scenarios with an even larger number of different hypotheses and to generalize their findings – speaking improves our brain activity and capability. Furthermore, speaking and listening allows us to absorb knowledge from others, which might have taken us a significantly longer time to learn by ourselves, which is the ultimate reason for the constant advance of the human race. Can you imagine a world where every new generation of people would have to start over? We would still be living in prehistoric times if that were the case. Luckily for civilization, it isn't and an argument can be made that speaking and listening are the two most important aspects of the human race, because, without them, nothing would exist in the way we know it today.

The same study conducted in 2013 also pointed out that there is a difference in the levels of a protein, synthesized in our brains, that essentially regulates how much we need to speak, between the two genders. That's not particularly important for our studies in this book, but it's an interesting fact that women have a need to speak, on average, a total of 20000 words per day, compared to a somewhat modest 7-10 thousand for men.

In the modern society we live in, communication determines everything that our lives revolve around – the jobs that we get, the people that we meet, the relationships that we have with those people. Without proper communication, we're dead in the water. There's a term that became quite popular in the past few years known as "networking", which refers to the building of relationships with people specifically for the sake of business. It would essentially dictate that we need to be acquaintances with as many people as possible and expand our network of business contacts. While this may be useful for some, it has recently been modified based on the understanding that humans are, above all, emotion-driven. We are much more likely to help a friend in need than someone who we simply know in our line of work. As a result, a new movement has emerged, which focusses on building actual relationships with people, which may be beneficial for business, but are also good for us as humans and all our other needs. It's been adopted by many of the Fortune 500 companies as their business model and I believe we should all adopt it as our own business model. A relationship is infinitely more valuable than someone you just know and whose phone number you have. Relationships revolve around personal treatment and value rather than just business interest. Furthermore, if relationships are built successfully, they eventually transform into friendships.

I would like to take a moment to emphasize the importance of friendship. Friends are not just people that you can call when you're feeling down or when you want to go out partying. A good friend will help you achieve your dreams by providing positive stimulus when you need it, they will offer a different perspective on a problem that you may have, not in a way that makes them feel superior to you, but an attempt to actually provide a viable solution. They will be with you both in times of happiness and grief, for as long as your friendship exists. Furthermore, there are actual health benefits to having healthy friendships – certain studies have shown that having close friends can lead to reduced stress levels, which is especially important in our otherwise extremely stressful lives and boost your self-esteem at the same time. When talking about business, my golden rule to creating relationships, both with customers and partners, is to provide value and to never think you are irreplaceable. The same principles apply to communication between people without the business being involved. As long as you consistently provide value to your customers or friends, you will retain those relationships and improve on them with every single encounter. There are a few tips that I like using in my personal relationships that have helped me build a vast network of friends, who are always willing to help me out and, of course, I would do the same for them. Here are some of them:

1. Choose your friends wisely – this doesn't include your closest friends, the ones that you drink your beer with on a Sunday afternoon, but rather those

who are somehow related to your business or work. Make sure you're always choosing people who can provide value back to you so that you don't end up giving away too much for nothing in return.

2. Think before you speak, especially when specific views are involved. You wouldn't want to insult someone on their religious, cultural or whatever other beliefs they may have. Remember to always stay neutral in conversations that involve any sort of beliefs.

3. Don't try to solve everybody's problems or give advice when it's not asked for – a mistake many people make over and over again is to give advice to their friends, without being asked for it. They simply believe that since the other person is sharing a situation or an issue they need advice, which is not always the case. If someone wants your advice, they will ask for it specifically.

4. Show your gratitude for them – never take anyone for granted, ever. They simply aren't and people might feel that way without you even knowing it. That's why I believe it's best to show

them how much they really mean to you by a small gesture every now and then. It doesn't have to mean that you have to buy them anything expensive, or anything at all. Sometimes a simple: "Hi, how are you?" will do the trick.

5. Make your word worth something – people give their word far too often, which results in it gradually losing value over time. When you make a promise to someone, make sure you can keep that promise before committing to it. Once you've committed, do everything in your power to fulfill that promise, so that the next time you're asked for something your promise isn't just a word.

Personal friendships are a bit more complicated, especially when we get into the topic of close friends. It can sometimes be misleading to believe that a certain friendship is healthy, just like with relationships. Unfortunately, however, that's not always the case and some people can mislead you into believing they are your friends, but, in fact, have dishonest intentions. I've witnessed many such cases throughout my life and my fair share of terror that has come from them. One particular occasion that I can vividly remember involved a friend of mine, whom I am still in touch with to this day. Let's call him James to preserve his identity. James is an attorney, who graduated from a very prestigious university. He's been working for one of the top L.A. firms for over 15 years now. About 10 years ago, however, he met a rather interesting person. He was educated, extremely well-spoken and had this exceptional charm about him. I can't remember his name, but let's call him Dave. Dave spent the better part of a year bonding with James, during which time I was constantly advising him to be careful since he was too pushy about their interactions. One day, James called and informed me that Dave and he had started a new business together, which involved the production of oak wood in a sustainable way. The business plan was elaborate, extremely well created and believable. In fact, it was a great idea – even the timing was perfect. There were government subsidy documents involved and an extremely large upfront investment of close to $250k each. I was initially extremely happy for James and, against my better judgment, I congratulated him on the new business and wished him the best of luck. They spent another month or so planning out the specifics of how they were going to secure the government subsidies in question and setting up all the legal documentation for the business. After it was all done, Dave was supposed to leave on a business trip to D.C, where he would negotiate with someone else, who was doing a similar thing, to obtain some valuable information about the specifics of growing the trees themselves. Given that the trip was supposed to take a week, James started calling Dave after the 7 days were up, asking why he hadn't returned yet. Many excuses and a month later, Dave was nowhere to be found and James decided to run a background check on him. It turned out that he had died 20 years ago and someone had assumed his identity. James was scammed, by a con-artist of the highest order, who managed to persuade and fool a very well-educated and smart man into giving them 250k of their own money. This story, although tragic, should serve as an example that no one is ever immune to being fooled, which is why it's important to know what true friendship looks like and what are the potential red flags to look out for.

1. Always be aware of new people who appear into your life without you specifically looking for them, who seem to be a perfect match with you. I'm not saying that such an event is impossible to be genuine, but just be careful. There are a lot of people that are up to no good in this world and will do everything in their power to take what's yours.

2. If you ever get an alarm signal in your brain saying that something's wrong, don't ignore it. It's your subconscious telling you that there's something fishy going on. Do some research and find out if it was a false alarm or there was, in fact, something to be worried about.

3. A true friendship should be filled with support, not competition. Friends don't have to compete with one another, they could, if that's their thing, but competition should always be friendly. Any time that you catch a friend of yours trying to one-up you, either stop competing or find better friends.

4. Trust should be a pivotal point for every relationship. It's the superior form of human interaction, when you choose to share personal information with others and, hopefully, they will keep it confidential and not share it with other people without your permission.

5. Feeling good – this is a great way to tell if someone really is your friend – every time that you spend time with them and leave, you should feel great, amazing even. If you feel anxious or like you could've beaten them, this is not a friendship, but a rivalry.

Obviously, friendships are a two-way relationship. They are built on mutual trust, mutual respect and a sense of security. There are a great number of ways that you can ruin your friendship in a small fraction of the time it took you to build it, leaving nothing behind, but a sour taste in everyone's mouth. Here are some of the things you should avoid at all costs:

1. Betraying your friend's trust — betraying someone's trust can be done in a number of ways, but from my experience, the most hurtful ones involve personal matters. For example, if a friend shares some information with you about an insecurity they might have, or a problem in their current relationship, don't ever break the confidentiality of your friendship by giving that information to someone else. You might think that this will help them in some way, and even if it does, they still are very likely to be upset about your actions.

2. Gossip — we've spoken about gossip already, but I feel like I should emphasize on it again, because friends are very likely to gossip about each other. Especially when you're a part of some sort of a group of friends, it's common to see each member talking about another behind their back in the company of the others. It's not a pleasant experience and although everyone thinks nobody speaks about them — the minute they're gone they're also the topic of discussion.

3. Lying – once again, we've discussed this earlier, yet it's so important. Don't lie to your friends, this is just another way for you to break their trust and ruin your relationship. Think about the last conversation that you had. Now think about all the times you were suspicious about being lied to. I couldn't think of a single one, because my last conversation was with a friend and that's how it's supposed to be. Now imagine the same conversation, only the things that person said were lies – everything changes instantly, doesn't it? That's because when communicating with friends or people that we trust, in general, we don't even think about being lied to. Although this makes us vulnerable, since our guard is down, that's rather the point of having friends in the first place, so make sure you don't exploit that vulnerability at all costs. If you've done something wrong and have to admit it – do so, it will be infinitely better than lying about it.

4. Not caring – although this won't break your friendship instantly, it will – over time. Friends aren't people that we just get, we have to work

for those friendships, constantly. Therefore, the moment that the other person starts feeling neglected, they're likely to reduce the amount of time they spend with you and gradually your relationship will fade into the "used to be" status.

Friendships and connections make us who we are as people, more than we care to admit. We've all heard the saying that you become who you surround yourself with and it's absolutely true. We adapt and learn from our environment, mostly from other humans, which is all the more reason we should choose wisely and have control over our relationships. Be a good friend and you'll expand your social circle dramatically, which, in turn, will pay you back in many shared experiences and good memories. This brings us to your final point in this book, which we'll discuss in the next chapter.

ASSET 9 – APPLICATION AND BREAKING FREE FROM YOUR COMFORT ZONE

I feel like we've talked a fair bit about how to improve your social skills in terms of actionable steps, therefore this chapter is going to be focused on creating the incentive to go out and practice what you have learned so far. I'm not saying that you haven't learned anything, just that I hope you've been paying attention. I'm a big fan of the practice, my mother always used to tell me that practice makes perfect and she was right (aren't mothers always right?). Nothing comes easy in life, not money, not success, not happiness, but I will do my best to break things down as much as possible for you to make practicing easy.

Let's dive in.

I'd like to present my favorite methods before I dive into some of the more scientific stuff on how to efficiently practice something. Researchers say you need ten thousand hours to master a skill, but hey, we've got a head start. We've only been practicing those skills since the day we were born. Maybe we've had them a bit wrong, but that can be corrected.

I have a special fondness for arguments. There's something so sexy about proving a point through facts and proper expression of those facts that can't beat anything else in terms of social skill practice in my opinion. So what do I do? I go to a debate club. You know, like the ones in high school? Well, turns out there are adult versions, too. Whoever thought of that, thank you. Although this may be my own personal preference, there is a lot to be said about debate clubs that proves a really strong point. Get it? A strong point for arguments? Nerdy joke, ha-ha, but nevertheless, these clubs are amazing. They involve communication of the highest level, where you're required to conform to the social rules set by the particular club, you have to learn patience and listening because you can't possibly fight your opponent if you haven't heard what they're saying and well, interrupting isn't allowed. They teach you restraint because regardless of how personal you may feel a particular case is, it really isn't about that at all. A discussion is just that, period. Perhaps the best part is that it's an absolute must for you speak clearly, confidently and think your way out of situations that you don't often encounter in real life. Essentially, it's a sandbox simulation of conflict in life, only with words, not fists or guns and if you fail you don't die, you just try again, and again, and again until you begin understanding the true importance of social skills and how a person with a good command of them can influence literally every situation.

Maybe you're not a fan of debate clubs or you don't have one available nearby, whatever the case may be, fear not, we have alternatives for you.

Get a part-time job as a salesman. This is amazing, honestly. Especially nowadays where you can be a salesman from the comfort of your home in your pajamas? And earn a little extra cash on the side? Being a salesman is something that I would recommend to anybody, regardless of their current background, unless it is sales, of course. And I would advise it to be a full-time occupation for a while, but not everyone is 20 years old and has a lot of free time. A career in sales is definitely not for everyone, but it forces you to go out there and talk to people, practice your social skills and you have a direct incentive to improve them – you will earn more money. Other similar jobs that I would recommend are waiters, bartenders, promoters and basically any job that pays for you to talk to people. As I said, it doesn't have to be full-time, you don't have to give up your entire career, but believe me, it will make all the difference in the world.

I feel like I've talked enough about bars already, so I'm going to suggest a different avenue of meeting people this time. Try charity work. Charity brings people together under the same cause and is often so diverse in terms of the people that participate. You can see anyone from a car salesman to a CEO at a charity event and, just like the hobby clubs we spoke about in the previous chapters, you get a pre-prepared topic to talk about. Although I would not recommend going to charity events with the sole purpose of meeting new people and not caring about why those people are actually there. If you want to do some good, pick a cause that resonates best with you and go to one of their events, you're sure to meet at least a few people, who are there for the same reasons. I met one of my early business partners at a charity event. Although I went because my wife insisted, I actually had a great time and got to meet a lot of new people, one of which became a very dear friend of mine and eventually we became business partners. It may not work the first time and it may feel uncomfortable, too. That's why it's always a great idea to bring a friend, especially if you've never been to such an event before. Having someone that you know will help you feel more secure and not the odd-one-out.

You could also always go to a work-related seminar. Not only will this provide ample opportunity for you to improve your career skills, but you are 100% guaranteed to find people with similar interests to yours. There are a few tips that I will share about going to seminars that will be extremely valuable if you decide to go to one:

1. Research who's going to be there – usually, larger seminars have publicly available attendance lists, where you can research who's going to show up and possibly find someone that is occupying the exact same position you are trying to get. This will allow you to approach that person directly and interact with them as a person who wants to follow their path. Most people are really open to mentoring others and will gladly share their experience and industry-specific tips of their own.

2. If you can't find someone who's really closely related to your niche, go for the next best. Don't be afraid to talk to people at seminars – they're there to exchange experience and learn, just like you. There's nothing shameful in asking for advice and you can even use this tactic as an approach, regardless of whether the person has any experience valuable to you. Once again, people are generally open to mentoring and open up much more if they believe you want to learn from them and look up to them, in a way.

3. Bring a friend, if you can. This is especially helpful if you work in a larger company since it's likely that one of your colleagues will gladly join you on a business trip to improve their skills as well. The benefit of doing that is this you can set up a list of people that you want to talk to and divide them up between the two of you, sharing your experiences at the end.

4. Ask your company to pay for your trip – most companies will have a budget for education purposes and that budget is not usually 100% expanded. This means that they always leave the opportunity to fund an ambitious employee, who has shown interest in a particular field, related to their work. This will not only save you the expenses that you would otherwise have to cover yourself but will put you on the map for promotion, since your seniors will know you're trying to improve and are willing to go the extra mile.

Finally, I would like to mention any pet-related activities, which although not useful for everyone, can be a delight for the ones that own pets. You don't have to go to a pet show to meet other people with similar interests to yours, you could always go to the local park. Most often, there will be a small group of people who assemble at the local park to spend some time outside with their pets. I've seen cats, dogs, foxes and pretty much everything in between at my park, but it's generally a very pleasant experience. They're guaranteed to welcome you warmly, because they love animals as much as you do. Then you'll have plenty of time to talk about things that you'll for certain be interested in if you own a pet, while your pet will have opportunity to socialize and play, as well. If you don't own a pet, I would seriously consider getting one. Pets have been linked to reduced stress and anxiety, as well as showing some signs of reduced risk for cardiovascular disease. The benefits far outweigh the drawbacks, well, for me at least. Be careful with your choice though and always make sure that you can dedicate yourself to this animal, they're just like a child in many ways. Don't rush that decision, read some literature on which breeds are suitable to your specific lifestyle and needs and make an informed decision. You won't regret it, I promise.

Science has also helped us understand how improving any skill works in general. In the following list, I'm going to share some of my personal favorites on the subject:

1. Get invested – that's right, motivation comes first and it's always the pivotal point for you to start doing anything. However, being motivated and being invested into something are two different things. To properly master a skill, you need to put the time in and go out and practice the techniques required and over time, you will improve.

2. Never use talent as an excuse – This is especially important in the topic discussed in this book, since many people use character traits as reasoning for having poor social skills. For example, you might hear that some is great at communicating with others, because they're extroverted, which is simply not true. Being intro- or extroverted has an impact on how many people you would choose to communicate with and your general level of involvement, but it won't determine whether you're good at it. I know many introverted people, who have great

communicational skills, yet prefer to keep to themselves for the most time and many extroverted people, who constantly seek new people to socialize with and fail miserably, because they lack the skills.

3. Set specific goals – I've sort of taken the liberty to do this for you by defining the chapters of this book, but that doesn't mean there isn't any room for improvement – break the components down even further, digest them in your own way and come up with your own ways of practicing the techniques. Keep in mind though, that the more realistic goals you set for yourself, the more likely you are to achieve them and avoid being disappointed with yourself.

4. Have a support system – much like a business, which needs a customer support department, you need to have a supportive environment to improve your skills. Research shows that positive reinforcement is key for general success. Your support network should mostly be comprised of your closest friends, who are going to be there for you throughout the process, give you adequate

feedback on how you're doing and possibly provide their insight on the topic as well.

5. Use mnemonics techniques – Mnemonics is a field of psychology which studies the way we memorize things. More specifically, they study how to improve your cognitive ability and memory. There are plenty of techniques developed by now, each more suitable for a specific set of tasks. Although mnemonic techniques are typically used for different skills than social, such as learning new languages, mathematics, general memory, etc. they can be equally as useful on your quest to social skill improvements. A few of them are in my arsenal at all times to help me in difficult situations, and I will share them with you

    5.1 The first technique that I like to use has not been created by a scientist, but by a writer, no other but Arthur Conan Doyle. In his famous work on the character Sherlock Holmes, he mentions that Holmes uses an imaginary place, known as the Mind Palace, to store information using a very specific set of mnemonic tools to find that information on demand. Although mnemonics wasn't really a field of study in his time, the author managed to come up with this concept, which explains why it's really hard to find any information on it. However, the mind palace, for lack of better word, is a tool that I use in a number of ways. Not only can it be used in the traditional fashion to store information in a systematic way and access it on demand, but it can also serve as your own personal refuge. I like retreating to my mind palace when visualizing, as it helps me concentrate my attention and imagination. To use the mind palace, one must first create it – as the word says, the palace can be any sort of a home, whether it's a palace or a garden shed is irrelevant. If you choose to use this technique to help you memorize anything that you want to, I suggest that you create your mind palace by visualizing a location that is very familiar to you, since the more familiar the place and the more detail you can remember about it, the more information you would be able to store. It works rather simply – for example you want to remember that your brother's birthday is on the 23rd of June. You go inside your mind palace and find some sort of a container – a small box – and you write the date on a piece of paper. You then put the piece of paper in the box and walk away. The next time you look in the box you will find the piece of paper still there, with the date written on it.

If you choose to use the mind palace to visualize, you can create an entirely imaginary place. Once again, the more detail that you create, the better. I choose to use the palace to visualize, mostly because I find it extremely difficult to concentrate when most of my days are spent with my cellphone buzzing all the time, someone talking to me and at the end of the day I'm exhausted and wired. Then I retreat to my mind palace for a while and I evaluate the day's progress and create a plan for the next day. The more that you practice accessing your mind palace, the easier it will be to get in and the more information you will be able to store. Honestly, I can't say enough great things about the mind palace, it has helped me tremendously over the years in all sorts of difficult situations. Keep in mind, though, that this technique requires plenty of practice and is not generally easy to master, but no things in life worth having is easy to get.

5.2   The second tool in my arsenal of mnemonic techniques is what's known as the "crazy tale". A rather simple, yet terrifically effective trick in my books. The crazy tale is a short story that you make up when you have to remember some key pieces of information and don't have time to write them down or the moment isn't convenient for you to do so. For example, if you have to give a speech you could use the crazy tale instead of a note for your bullet points or when you're meeting someone new and want to remember important things such as their name, age, occupation, etc. The way it works is simple – you make up a short story that has a consistent flow in advance. The best way to do this is by imagining a walk – I like walking through the woods, for example. Then, you add objects as you go along and create absurd word combinations to help you remember that information. For example, let's say you want to remember the name of Tristan, whom you just met, who's a carpenter, 34 years of age and is married to Tina. The story, for me would look something like this: "I was walking through the woods one day. I went past the house of Red Riding Hood and inside it was Tristan, dressed in knight's gear. He was working on a piece of wood, but he was using an inflatable mallet to hit it, which wasn't doing too much. On that piece of wood was written that $3+4=9$, which is obviously wrong. I left and continued on my way, but then Tina, dressed in a wolf's costume told me to wait. Silly as it may seem, the more absurd the word combinations, the easier they are to remember and you can still remember those words for up to 20! days after the initial story was created. When practicing this skill, make sure to start small, is in our example, with 4-5 words and work your way up. Eventually, you can remember upwards of 100 words, but it does require a pretty long walk.

Now breaking free from your comfort zone is slightly more difficult to do. First, you have to understand where your comfort zone's boundaries are and what they're holding you back from. For example, during my early days in university, which I've talked about earlier, my comfort zone was extremely tight and practically every social encounter represented a potential problem for me. Over time, as my social skills improved, so did my tolerance for new scenarios and unexpected outcomes. I've noticed that this tends to happen with many people, as we get into our 20's our comfort zones begin expanding, until about our 40's, when we're confident, we've got our lives under control, probably have a family and a few kids and then it begins shrinking back down again as we age. This is nothing to be afraid of, it's just a natural cycle. There are certain things that you can do to speed that process up and to force it, if you have to. I always recommend my clients to start small. Once you know where your boundaries are, make baby steps to go out of those boundaries by just a little bit, then come back to where you started and repeat, only take a larger step next time. This applies to any set of boundaries that you may have and that you may wish to expand.

You could, also, take a riskier approach by jumping into the deep and doing something that's extremely out of character for you and possibly regret making that decision in the first place. Keep in mind that although our time is a limited resource, life is a marathon, not a sprint and the more you train the better you'll become at it.

There are also plenty of social situations that you can get into by accident and I would advise you to take every single opportunity that you can and make the most of it. After all – time is our most valuable resource and wasting time is a sin. Go out there, explore, learn, educate yourself and soon enough you will not only be a master of social skills, but you will conquer life as a whole.

CONCLUSION

When I started writing this book I set out to make an impact. I wanted to make sure that my knowledge was available to anyone who was willing to learn and I believe I've achieved that. We've talked about all the different aspects of socials skills, how to improve on them and what you can expect to happen once you do so. Personally, I would say that if I had this book when I started learning about social skills, life would've been a whole lot easier for me at the time. What we haven't mentioned yet is how important I believe it is for you to follow your own path. I've made sure that my experience in life was narrowed down into this rather short book and transformed into something like a guide for people to look at, yet I feel that the most important part of my message was neglected. I could go on talking about myself, but it's time we spoke about you, my fellow readers. If there's one single piece of advice I could give someone and make sure that it's as impactful as possible, it would be to go out of your way to be yourself. Never let anyone tell you otherwise. Don't let people bring you down, because their beliefs somehow differ from yours, or they feel superior to you or they have better social skills that you. Use such occasions as motivation for your own personal improvement. Hold your head up high in every situation, because every person on this planet is special in their own way and you're no different. Never forget that you can always improve your current situation, regardless of how grim things may seem at times and your social skills will be the perfect addition to the new you. Don't allow yourself to be caught up in the trappings of society and go down a path you're not certain you want to walk. Always take the time to analyze where making a certain decision will take you, hopefully this book will help you do that more clearly. Set clear values for yourself, even if you think you've got yours in control, take the time to revise and update them, and do so on a regular basis to ensure you're always on the right track. Do the same with your goals, both in terms of practicing the concepts I've outlined in this book and for everything else in life. Value your current relationships and always strive to build new ones, but always be as cautious as you can be that you don't make the mistakes we've showcased. If there is a person that you love, say so and don't risk losing them, just because you were too busy doing something else.

Furthermore, I would once again like to point out the importance that social skills play in our daily lives, just to give you that little extra motivation to go out of your way that extra mile. Without doubt social skills have been the primary key to success in my life and I consider myself to be successful. I wrote about the importance of social skill plenty in this book, but the one thing that I would like to mention once again are the statistics of the modern world. I briefly touched on a study done recently showing that people with a better command of social skills are much more likely to have a better career path that those with simply academic knowledge. Now that we've also discussed connections and friendships and how they all bind together to form this complex maze, that we have to navigate every day, known as society, we can understand why that study showed the results that it did.

Our world is changing exponentially faster with each year that goes by, largely thanks to technological advances. This rapidly changing environment means that we no longer stay as competitive as we used to 20 or 30 years ago once we graduate from some educational institution. Today, we walk out of college and our knowledge is already outdated, especially if we're involved in a new branch of science. This should only further emphasize on how important social skills really are. Without them, we're stuck in a cycle of educating ourselves more and more, yet never being competitive enough to get the right job. Chances are, though, that if you've created the relationships with the right people, you will be in the position to negotiate your dream job and make it happen. Or maybe it's not a job that you need, but a new friend to share your life with.

Regardless of the scenario and your goals at the time, social skills are a tool that the modern person needs, I dare say, more than any other, which is all the more reason for everyone to get involved in improving their own set and helping their friends and relatives do the same, too. I wish you all the best of luck on your journey to success in life, however you choose to define it.

Most importantly, strive to be as happy as you can be.

Yours sincerely,

Damien Reed.

RESOURCES

Fox2p protein, ghr.nlm.nih.gov

A.Paivio, A.Desrochers (1981) – mnemonic techniques in learning

A.Alesina (1989)– Public confidence

G.Overbeek, AHN Cillessen, RCME Engels(2012) – a longitudinal study of the associations among adolescent conflict resolution styles, depressive symptoms and romantic relationship longevity